MONEYWING$™

Unfolding Your Financial Potential
One Brave Feather At A Time

Marlene Elizabeth, M.Ed.

RHG | MEDIA PRODUCTIONS™

TABLE OF CONTENTS

Acknowledgements

Giving birth to my daughter late in life after two grueling days of labor was much easier for me than giving birth to my life-long dream of writing this book. I'm thrilled and incredibly thankful to everyone who has been "the wind beneath my wings" to unfold this dream.

Thank you from the bottom of my heart to my beautiful participants and clients who have shown up and said "yes" to this work. Thank you for your courage and trust in me. It's been an honor to walk beside you. From the earliest phase to the present stage of **MONEYWINGS™**, I'm so thankful for your valuable engagement, feedback, and suggestions that have helped this work become what it is today.

To all my esteemed professors and fellow U.S. and International students at my wonderful Religious Education graduate program at Boston College School of Theology and Ministry - thank you for fanning my spiritual gifts into a flame. My deepest appreciation to my spiritual director Sr. Dolores - your deep compassion, tender spirit and faith deeply blessed me to feel comfortable in my own skin.

To my admired money mentor Deborah Price: Thank you for providing me with the powerful tools to support others in their relationship to money. I'm proud to be part of your Money Coaching Institute community. You arrived into my life at the time I most needed support. Thank you for your faith, trust and loving spirit that welcomed me with open arms.

To my dear mentor, Julie Anderson, who introduced me to the powerful world of our brain personality connection. I'm immensely grateful to you and the life-changing knowledge you've equipped me with to share with my community.

To my phenomenal mentor and publisher, Rebecca Hall Gruyter / RHG publications and her awesome team: Thank you for so lovingly and powerfully empowering me to share my vision and voice in the world. I'm eternally grateful for your guidance, leadership, expertise and faith which reflects the heart of **MONEYWINGS™**.

To Monique Feil Photography: Thank you for sharing your gorgeous creative talent and capturing the photo that became the cover for this book.

To my beloved parents: Thank you for cultivating in me the belief that I can do anything; always being there to support my life's adventures; and nurturing the value of education and life-long learning. Because of you, I'm blessed to share hope that more is possible.

To my cherished Grandma Tina: Thank you for being my role model for faith and finances. Everything I've learned from you carries on in me, my daughter and the future generations of our family tree. I am deeply grateful and blessed to be your granddaughter.

To my treasured friends: Sandra - I am grateful beyond words. In my wildest dreams, there could be no better friend in life than you. Your life has richly taught me about humility - that humility is not thinking less of yourself. It's thinking of yourself less. Thank you for teaching me this backbone of a person's relationship to money. Kim - thank you for nearly four decades of steadfast love and faith in me. It is a dream-come-true celebrating a book that you always knew existed in me. I'm grateful to each and every moment of your support. Cherri - God made you and broke the mold. I'm so thankful for your beautiful friendship and for the powerful feminine role-model you are in the world of faith and finances. I'm grateful to each one of you who have always cheered me on, believed in me, never left my side as you patiently waited for this late-bloomer to fly.

No words could express my deepest appreciation for my precious, amazing daughter Dalena. I am so lucky to be your Mama. Thank you for the world of tenderness and joy you have brought to my life. Thank you for inspiring me to grow **MONEYWINGS™**. May everything I've shared in this book remind you -- and all of us - that love is greater than fear and that we never, ever walk alone. I am with you always.

With hands extended, I give you thanks above all God for the gift and grace of **MONEYWINGS™**. May it abundantly bless all those you lead to discover it.

Foreword

When I first met Marlene, I was impressed by her integrity, authenticity, warmth, and her commitment to helping others. I was also struck by her deep love for her daughter and her willingness to step forward no matter what …to become all her daughter believes her to be and believes her to be capable of bringing to the world.

As I have gotten to know Marlene on deeper levels, I have discovered those first impressions have proven true. I can add to the list an incredible heart, mind, and gifting to help other women in a very positive and uplifting manner. And, her deep care of her daughter that inspired Marlene to grow her own **MONEYWINGS™** for herself and now bringing it to the world so that we can all grow our own beautiful wings, one brave feather at a time.

We (RHG Media Productions & RHG Publishing) are truly honored to partner with Marlene Elizabeth to bring her transformational book to the world. What an honor and privilege to be selected as the publishing company to share out this empowering book. Personally, I am truly honored to know Marlene, and I know that this book will uplift you and empower you to grow your own **MONEYWINGS™** so that you can soar!

Her subject of supporting women around money is one that is close to my heart. My background includes working in the financial and business industries for over fifteen years. I empowered start-up companies to Fortune 500 companies and their employees, running a successful and thriving private practice achieving the circle of champions multiple times and the $25 Million-dollar club. I found even with my rich background and experience in the Financial Industry, she shared some powerful questions and ways to look at things that touched and expanded my wings too.

As an Empowerment Leader, Publisher, Author, Network Owner, Business Coach, Speaker and Publisher.... my team and I are in the business of uplifting people around the world...one heart and life at a time. This is exactly what Marlene is doing with her powerful book...as she supports people in building their own powerful and positive relationship with money...she is impacting heart by heart, life by life, family by family, community by community, state by state, and country by country. We celebrate her bringing her light, knowledge and inspiration around money.

I celebrate you leaning in and saying yes to this book...as I know it will bring powerful transformation into your life. I know you will be equipped, encouraged, uplifted, and empowered to build your own powerful **MONEYWINGS™.** As you build your beautiful wings, may you feel Marlene's beautiful encouragement as the wind beneath your wings and SOAR!

Rebecca Hall Gruyter, Empowerment Leader Committed to helping you make a positive difference around the world…one heart and life at a time!

CEO of RHG Media Productions, RHG TV Network, and Your Purpose Driven Practice.

www.YourPurposeDrivenPractice.com
www.RHGTVNetwork.com
Rebecca@YourPurposeDrivenPractice.com

(925) 787-1572

Introduction

"...freedom is sometimes just simply another perspective away; who could you be if your lens was changed for a moment, would you still be the same?"

- "Perspectives" by Kutless

When my daughter turned four, I took a leap from the nest of my comfort zone to spread my entrepreneurial wings for the first time.

It was the start of the most daring, richest and grueling three years of my life.

I set out to achieve my financial dream to raise a money-smart girl as a stay-at-home single-Mom. I had no idea that my broken relationship to money would prevent my dream from ever taking flight.

I didn't even know what "a relationship with money" meant, much less that this would result in my having to admit to all the aspects of it - the good, the bad AND the ugly. My strengths and weaknesses. Courage and shame. All of it. I'll be honest. I felt scared and angry. I remember capturing my feelings that night in my journal:

Money is part of almost every aspect of our lives, so why is it that nobody thought it was important enough to teach us about it in school? Most important, how do I help my daughter to fly when I haven't even learned how to unfold my own money wings?

As this question plagued my spirit, it also triggered the memory of a quote I'd read during my religious education studies in grad school at Boston College:

"Be patient toward all that is unsolved in your heart and try to love the questions themselves... Live the questions now. Perhaps you will then gradually, without noticing it, live along some distant day into the answer."

- Rainer Maria Rilke

I made a bold decision to start living the question. Along the way, I discovered something very important. Living the question rather than trying to force the answer, unfolds the new story you wish to live. You start to focus on the "why" and soon find yourself living the "how."

Looking at money from a different perspective is how everything changed for me.

Today I am a successful mama-preneur, bestselling author, speaker, podcast host and the creator of **MONEYWINGS™** (published on my daughter's birthday who inspired this epic journey) with my next book on financial self-care due for release in 2019.

What is **MONEYWINGS™**? It's a new and dynamic way to look at your relationship to money. Growing money wings empowered me to break through my money challenges and unfold my financial dream one brave feather at a time. Just as **MONEYWINGS™** was life-changing for me, it can change the course of your financial future too.

As a certified money coach, brain personality specialist, and spiritual teacher, I love helping women see money differently so they can stop doubting and start unfolding their beautiful financial dreams.

The insights and strategies in this guide are designed to help you figure out what is standing in your way of finding financial success. What is holding you back?

It is filled with triumphant money stories, practical exercises and a safe, gentle, nurturing space for growing in your relationship to money. Each chapter reflects the values I hold dear -- compassion, excellence, beauty, integrity and faith.

After reading this book, you will never look at money the same way. We will explore money through a variety of lenses including spiritual, emotional, psychological, unique feminine power, and your brain personality. This is **MONEYWINGS™!**

When my daughter was in 1st grade, we discovered an educational TV program called *The Magic School Bus*. In one episode, the bus travels inside the human body for a "behind-the-scenes" view of what we only see from the outside.

In the same way, **MONEYWINGS™** helps you travel beyond the physical dollars and cents of personal finance into the inner-life of your money story - your money beliefs, experiences, history, habits, values, unique gifts and feminine strengths and so much more - to help you understand the inner dynamics of your actions around money.

How do you think about money? How do you react to it? How do you communicate about money? Your money story is foundational to how you see money.

If money was a subject of conflict in your house when you were growing up, your natural instinct may be to run and hide every time the subject comes up. If you avoid money conversations or play ostrich refusing to admit you have money problems, this could explain why.

Perhaps your memories of money growing up are associated with shame. One of my clients remembers standing in a grocery line with her mother, dreading the moment that always seemed to come when she realized she didn't have enough money. She could recall feeling a knot in the pit of her stomach embarrassed at the strangers watching.

These are real stories, with real consequences. While they are part of our childhood, they don't remain there. These experiences are woven tightly into our money story as adults. They remain there influencing every money decision we make until we muster the courage to break free of them, one brave feather at a time.

Here's the Good News! You have the power to re-write your money story. It no longer has to be a roadblock to your money dream.

There are so many different types of money dreams: Dreams of being the CEO and boss of your own business, creating a non-profit that serves an under-served population, putting your children through college, buying your first home or dream home, paying off debt, having a secure retirement or retiring early, making a seven-figure income, taking a dream vacation, going back to school, being a philanthropist or perhaps having an idea that will change the world (and generate a healthy revenue).

What's yours? Are you struggling to make your beautiful money dream come true?

Whatever your financial challenges may be, please know you are not alone! Let this book be your encouraging companion for the support you deserve to unfold your financial potential.

Success is a team-effort. To this day, I continue to expand my awareness through the mentoring and support of several beautiful, financially successful, heart-centered leaders and coaches who have inspired my work, as you'll see throughout the book. This guide is a small way I have chosen to pay forward my gratitude for all the help and support I have received along the way.

Find your cozy seat, indulge yourself with a soothing treat and enjoy a life-changing view of your relationship to money.

Chapter One
Fanning The Flame Of Your Financial Dream

"A comfort zone is a beautiful place, but nothing ever grows there."
- Unknown

Brimming with excitement, I pursued my financial dream and started my own business, doing what I love, as the boss of my own time, talent and income. I was in control, or so I thought.

Over the course of three years, I invested in business and personal development valued at over $20,000 with cash I didn't have to spend. But it takes money to make money, right? After all, I had lots of financial catch-up to do so I set the stage to make a big income... never mind that I'd never experienced earning more than $36,000 in a year.

I convinced myself that all I needed was the right training, certification and visibility to create the life I'd always imagined!

I pushed through neck and back pain caused by hours and hours slumped over my laptop creating my business plan, marketing materials and client programs.

Before long, I was putting housework off (not for a few days, but a few years) while struggling as a single Mom to make ends meet.

I poured precious energy, focus and time into my financial dream, working so hard I couldn't remember the last time I'd eaten, or even showered.

My heart ached as my daughter re-played baby videos of mommy spending time with her. We no longer had time to play. I was beginning to sound like a broken record, "Not now honey." "I can't right now, sweetie. I have to work."

Knowing first-hand the years spent struggling to reach my financial dream, my best-friend of 25 years who believed in me more than I believed in myself, cheered me on as we both privately worried that if I didn't succeed for the up-teenth time, I probably never would.

Just as I was about to give up, I landed my first client which sent my spirit soaring. When I cashed that first payment, the pure bliss of generating my own income washed over me like sweet rain. I did a happy-dance and celebrated with my daughter as each new client enrolled...$500... $800... $1,000... $2,000...

Yes! I can do this! I'm really going to do it. This time, I'm going to fly!

But I never did fly.

My business was burning up cash as quickly as it was coming in. Exhaustion and frustration began to set in as I tried to manage all the moving parts of my new enterprise alone – from marketing to business education and development, to the actual work of my clients, to customer service and administrative tasks – all of it.

Spinning my wheels and going nowhere fast, I remained stuck in the same place where I had started.

Except, not exactly. My finances and self-care suffered worse than when I started my journey to create a better life.

Above all, I missed spending precious time with my daughter.

Surely, doing something meaningful that I loved shouldn't be this hard! I racked my brain, unable to understand what I was doing wrong.

What magic ingredient was I missing?

What more did I need to do to succeed?

I sunk my head into my hands and closed my eyes. The memory of a lighter scene appeared in my mind of me laughing with my daughter during the opening act of *Shrek the Musical.* In the scene, Shrek's parents have a message for him on his 7th birthday:

It's a big, bright, beautiful world
With happiness all around
It's peaches and cream And every dream comes true—
But. Not. For. You.

Why did financial dreams seem so easy for others to build, but not for me? Oh my gosh! I was developing a Shrek complex! :)

I desperately reached for a life-line in my mind and remembered my friend's voice saying, "Don't give up." My own feeble inner-voice pushed, "Just try Marlene... get up one more time and try again. You can stay in bed and never know, or you can get up right now and just try!"

But none of this made an impact -- until I thought of my daughter sleeping peacefully in the next room.

At that moment, one fact became crystal clear: She was my WHY who empowered me to get up instead of give-up.

Like solid, sweet-scented wax that keeps the candle-flame lit, her life gave me strength to rise above the negative self-talk. She was the WHY that kept me steady and gave me the strength to finally face my relationship to money head-on.

Brave-Heart Tip: Know your COMPELLING WHY behind your financial dream. It will become your anchor when the winds of despair appear, and your life seems to be spinning out of control.

Your WHY will keep you from drifting aimlessly and giving up. Once you are able to re-focus on your WHY, you can hoist your sails, adjust for the wind and travel through each challenge ahead.

I'll be honest. For a few moments, I agreed with my fear and panic that the best solution was to climb back into my comfort zone where I felt safe. *What was I thinking! Who was I to try and be more, do more, have more? No wonder people settle for keeping things just the way they are, thank you very much!*

Until it dawned on me that was exactly the point. Giving birth to something new is never easy. I had chosen *not* to settle. That was the reason for the pain. I had dared to stretch beyond my comfort zone with faith, courage and hope. No wonder it all felt so messy! The truth is, new life comes with its growing pains.

This awareness put me back into the pilot's seat of my financial future. It helped me to stop being driven by fear and more by truth and love.

Brave Heart Tip: All the magic of your financial dream can only begin when you're willing to step beyond your comfort zone.

Anytime you stretch into something new, it is going to be uncomfortable. Expect it. But the Good News is the discomfort is temporary.

One morning, my daughter looked up from a piece of paper she had been intently focused on and said, "drawing eyes is hard!" Her Dad, who enjoys teaching her how to draw and paint, had dropped by for a visit. He replied, "Yes honey, it's not easy, or else everyone would be doing it."

Moving beyond our comfort zone to achieve our financial dream is not easy. It can trigger anxiety and panic. It can easily overwhelm us if we allow it. This brave work requires being patient and gentle with ourselves. It's very important to feel a sense of safety at deep levels throughout the course of building our dream.

The need for safety is powerfully captured in a scene from the musical Broadway production of *Beauty and the Beast.* When the villagers first see the Beast (the Prince) they are overcome by fear and sing, ***"we don't like what we don't understand, in fact it scares us"*** and off they go to "kill the beast!" (who, thanks to beautiful French furniture and dishes, is saved by love).

Tips For Restoring A Sense of Safety:

Feeling safe is at the core of our growth and sense of well-being. That's why along the journey of growing **MONEYWINGS™**, I fell in love with a few simple practices that powerfully cultivated a sense of safety and restored feelings of calm and security when things began to overwhelm me.

They are called somatic practices from Peter Levine's work on Somatic Experiencing® from his pioneering work in trauma therapy. Somatic means body-based. In a nut-shell, these practices gently give our bodies a feeling of safety no matter what's going on around us. Next time you feel unsettled or unsafe, try this:

Be Resourceful (Resourcing): Connect with an experience that supports a sense of trust and ease. For example, walk outside and take in nature. Soak in the sunshine. Notice the birds, trees and flowers. Light a favorite scented-candle, spend a little time with your animal friend. Play a special song. Draw strength and safety from your inner and external world.

Get Grounded (Grounding): Soothe your nervous system and ease anxiety by bringing awareness to your feet and the ground underneath them. Stand and feel the earth supporting you. If you are sitting, notice how your weight is fully supported. Exhale and inhale deeply slowly relaxing and letting go as you become consciously aware that the earth is always there supporting you.

Slowing Down (Titration): When your mind is racing, and anxiety starts to rise, you can restore a sense of calm by first returning back to the present moment where you are right inside your body. This is a powerful and effective practice to help your mind relax and re-center. Slowing down is also the practice of allowing yourself the time you need to integrate one tiny step at a time before taking your next tiny step (i.e., one brave feather at a time!) Feeling overwhelmed happens when we focus on taking the next ten steps. Therefore, focus on just taking one simple next step (and celebrate!).

Brave Heart Tip: Cultivating a sense of safety within yourself is essential for unfolding your financial dream.

I was willing to persist through the many challenges of mama-preneurship, in my devotion to empower my daughter to live *her* financial happy-ever-after, whatever she decides for it to be.

This is so often the case for women that their dreams arise to serve a greater purpose than merely for personal gain alone. My success is not about me at all. It's about my daughter's well-being. **Ironically, when it's no longer just about us, it becomes all about us. The universe begins to support our dream, in more ways than we imagined possible, helping us to make our vision a reality.**

Doors that were once firmly closed start to open. The right people begin to arrive in our lives to help us achieve our goals. We discover a check in the mail that we never expected. An opportunity arrives out of the blue and changes our lives forever. The rest is herstory.

What fuels your strength and courage to keep on loving and growing?

What keeps you from giving up, throwing in the towel, walking away from your dream?

Whatever it is, I encourage you to share it with another woman who might be struggling to follow her dream. The more we share our why and the purpose behind our dream, the more courageous we all become.

And if you are that person struggling, remember as Leonard Cohen sang,

"Ring the bells that still can ring. Forget your perfect offering. There is a crack in everything.
That's how the light gets in."

Experiencing freedom from fear takes time. And new fears surface just as soon as old ones fade away. So be very gentle and kind with yourself. Know that as they arise, you can release them and gain freedom so that you can soar!

Love has a way of persistently showing up, tugging at you like a child, encouraging you to choose life beyond your fears, again and again and again.

Let love ease the sorrow, anxiety and suffering that fear brings because the world needs your financial dream to come true. Your dream was placed in your heart for a purpose: to bring you joy and prosperity because it's something you'll excel at, and because it will contribute to the greater good.

Where is love tugging you to grow beyond your comfort zone today? What support do you need to start unfolding your dream?

As a strong, sometimes stubborn, independent woman, I was never comfortable reaching out for help. It always seemed easier to grind my way through challenges. I didn't realize that this mindset actually made life much harder, not easier at all.

Starting my own business required me to shift into a new mindset that was unfamiliar, but key to my success:

It's not only okay to reach out for support, it's *essential* for the big dreams, the big results, the big love you wish to pour into the world whether you own a business, or not.

Plus, it's way more fun! And fun is allowed ;)

As with any fear, the key to stepping beyond our comfort zone is tiny baby-steps. (And we're all in "baby phase" anytime we begin something new).

In addition to empowering my daughter, my dream is to help women share their love and gifts in their own unique way with the world.

The world needs the financial dream in your heart to come true.

I invite you to try these five tips to support you in unfolding your financial potential:

Trust your heart. Science proves that women are designed with incredible intuitive powers! There's wisdom dropped into us long before we understand it, but others can cause us to doubt it. When we follow our heart, "the how" will present itself along the way. This is what it means to "walk by faith, and not by sight."

Tend to your emotions with deep breaths and self-care. Stay present to the feelings that surface while working through your relationship to money. Light a candle. Read an inspiring quote or passage in a book. Write in your journal. Enjoy a warm shower or bath. Nibble dark-chocolate. Take a brief stroll. Call a supportive friend. Doodle. Mind-map. Watch an inspiring film. Engage positive, positive, positive self-talk… you get the idea. Be kind to yourself with compassion, self-forgiveness &gratitude.

Take tiny baby-steps in the direction of your financial dream. This is very important! Your "critter brain" needs proof all along the way that you will be A-OK as you shift into a new place in your life. So, always take small steps to experience small results, first, as you work your way steadily forward. If you jump in too far, too fast, your mind will kick into over-drive with all its fears, and doubts that are usually not even true, but will nevertheless work to keep you "safe" in what's familiar - safe, but unfulfilled because it will also keep you from realizing your full potential.

Find the support of a person or group for accountability and positive reinforcement that can help you reach your goals. Finding a community of like-minded women who share your values is vital to helping you get to where you're called to go. The richest groups share celebrations, successes, challenges and receive supportive feedback, including helpful resources, strategies and professional connections.

Treasure your financial dream. You might feel pressure inside and from people around you to stay small, even though you feel a strong desire to grow into something new (a new job or business, more income, etc.). When this happens, guilt, shame and doubt can set in. Instead, fan into a flame the gift of God, which is in you...the Spirit God gave you does not make you timid, but gives you power, love and self-discipline (2 Timothy 1:6- 7).

It takes big love to break through big fears that threaten the pursuit of our financial happy-ever-after.

But women show up with that big love, again and again. And miracles happen.

Fan the flame of your financial dream and watch the beautiful ways life transforms within in you and around you.

See you in the next chapter! :) xo Marlene

Chapter Two
Learning About Money Is Never Just About Money

"After more than 30 years in business, I am convinced that the difference in success and failure is not how you look, not how you dress, not how you're educated...
but how you think."

- Mac Anderson

Congratulations for showing up -- you've just added the first, beautiful brave-feather to your **MONEYWINGS™**! Whether in a favorite quill pen, spring bonnet, tiara, or fun fashion-hat, each brave feather is divine. I celebrate your courage and commitment to transform your money dream into reality.

No matter what your money dream is, **the most important first-step for take-off is confidence.** Without faith in ourselves, our money dreams will never have the necessary fuel to take flight. This is especially true when it comes to confidence in our relationship to money.

When we find ourselves stuck, I have learned that the reason is almost always due to what I call "invisible baggage" weighing us down. By this, I mean the hidden, subconscious money-beliefs we carry in our money story that often sabotages our financial success.

It is therefore so important to invest time in learning what you really believe about money, in order for your money dream to come true.

That's why I created the **Number Story,** one of my favorite exercises to help clients uncover their limiting money beliefs. Beginning with the numbers from their earliest years in life, to their current financial picture, they soon discover that their **numbers tell a money story.**

I designed Number Story after the experience of looking at my own numbers in a unique way which quickly and powerfully illuminated my limiting money beliefs.

Here's a behind-the-scenes view at how my Number Story unfolded for me, and how it can powerfully serve you too:

Step #1: List and describe three to five key ages from your early years that characterize proud moments, or positive experiences in your life that brought you joy. They can be very simple or detailed as you wish.

Here's a sample from my life:

Age Fourteen. A stadium-packed audience watched as I gently adjusted the microphone and cleared my throat to deliver a speech as ASB President on behalf of our junior-high graduating class.

Age Sixteen. The highway stretched out miles before us as my high-school friend and I fearlessly drove nine-and-a-half hours from California to Utah over Spring break to experience my first snow-ski lesson.

Age Nineteen. The jumbo jet sailed smoothly through the clouds as I flew alone, 3,000 miles away from home to Washington D.C. excited to begin an internship I'd earned with then, U.S. Congressman Leon Panetta.

Step #2: Notice the natural, positive strengths, characteristics or qualities that these experiences say about you and write them down in a sentence that starts with "I am....." How does it feel to hear these beliefs about yourself?

More often than not, you'll discover as I did that the age-numbers from the earliest times in your life say a whole lot about your authentic nature and zone of genius that contributes to the overall success in your life. In my case, ***I am confident, independent, smart and strong.*** I believe this about myself, and others see this in me too. With arms wide open, I positively embrace life with all its promise, adventure, opportunity and possibility for growth. I feel liberated and joyful expressing these words about myself.

Yet, something just never added up.

Why did my <u>financial numbers</u> tell a different tale - compared to the strengths and shinier parts in the rest of my story? Perhaps your own number story is telling a different story too that does not align with your positive strengths? If so...

Step #3: Gently, compassionately and honestly start unfolding your MONEY STORY, one small step at a time.

This is tender work. Please remember to extend forgiveness and extra self-care for yourself during this process. If you find yourself feeling overwhelmed, anxious or stuck, simply pause. Pay attention to your body and emotions and allow space to express your feelings, thoughts and physical sensations, as necessary. Return to your story as you are able. Please know that there is no right or wrong way to do this step. The most important practice is being as gentle with yourself as possible.

In my case, I'd earned not one, but two college degrees from excellent schools on both coasts at UC Davis in northern California and at Boston College, in my favorite U.S. city Boston, Massachusetts. I lived young and single in great health, with a deep faith in God, supportive family and friends, and with a courageous spirit.

Yet, I constantly struggled living paycheck-to-paycheck. None of it made any sense.

So, despite the limits of my income I earned in those first years of my young career, I spent beyond my means trying to keep up with the cost of uptown life in Orange County, CA -- one of the most expensive counties in the nation -- where I had been raised in an economically lower middle-class family household.

I found myself stuck on an endless merry-go-round of accumulating credit-card debt, then paying it off, and racking it all up again.

My self-esteem suffered and money shame started creeping in.

No matter how much I knew to avoid overdrafts and late fees, I'd still find them slipping onto my accounts anyway. Frustrated, I'd avoid looking at my bank statements, or simply leave them un-opened.

The idea of an emergency fund, retirement plan and life insurance coverage that people talked about sounded wonderful, and responsible. But in reality, those ideas also felt like foreign concepts, not to mention out of reach for someone like me who was paddling hard just to barely keep her financial nose above water.

I'd keep saying to myself that *I should know better... I should do better...* Other times, I felt so lost, I'd call out to the universe asking *where was I when God passed out* **MONEYWINGS™***?*

Strong women tend not to reach out for help. (Power tip: Smart women do!)

Instead, I avoided money conversations like bees in a garden. I'd distract and bury myself in loads of work, telling myself it would all sort itself out somehow, someway, someday.

Eventually without noticing, I got used to living a life of hiding my eyes away from all that hurt around my money challenges.

Before I knew it, years of valuable energy were spent quietly carrying my broken financial wings alone.

Until one day, from inside my own body, a miracle arrived, my daughter!

Her beautiful life fueled my courage and creativity to break through fears and doubts, renewing my faith to overcome my financial struggles.

Step #4: What is your compelling "*WHY*" that drives your money dream? Naming your why is powerful! Be sure to write it down.

If you're unable to name your persuasive reason, don't fret! Do your best to write something down, anyway. It will help you to get closer to unfolding your purpose soon. Uncovering your "why" can also empower you to take brave steps into the sacred ground that is your Money Story.

I realized that, much like my own parents, I didn't learn money management skills in school or at home. The money habits I developed arose solely from pure observation of those around me. Those habits became part of me without much thought, some positive, but mostly burdensome.

I dove into the waters of financial literacy learning all I could about building wealth, while privately questioning if I was smart enough to understand the foreign world of business and numbers. After all (I believed) "*I'm not good at math.*" Yet thanks to an excellent textbook I had found online, I discovered a valuable secret in the first few pages: Personal finance is not rocket science; it's about making positive, deliberate choices.

My real breakthrough came when I realized I'd been carrying invisible luggage into my relationship with money. I discovered that the conversation in my head looked vastly different than my typical positive beliefs in other areas of my life. **When it came to money, I believed: I am powerless, incompetent, helpless and fearful.**

I am generally a very positive and confident person. So, I was stunned to see that I subconsciously carried these hidden, negative beliefs about money. Yet at the same time, I also felt relieved that it all finally started to make sense!

The reason I struggled so long getting my business off the ground is because **we create what we believe.** I believed that wealth was not within my power to achieve or receive as a spiritual woman. As Robin S. Sharma points out: What we focus on grows. What we think about expands. My focus at that time was *you can't be spiritual and wealthy.* Without realizing it, I energized this belief and therefore, I struggled to achieve and receive wealth.

Which self-limiting belief do you feel you might be carrying into your relationship with money?

Step #5: W.A.T.C.H. and Create What You Believe

The final step of Number Story is my core and absolute favorite tool I teach for helping women heal their self-limiting money beliefs.

It's based on a simple, yet profound quote that was taped to the inside of our living room cupboard for three years until I realized the power it held. On a humble white sheet of paper, five sentences written in black, bold letters revealed timeless wisdom with roots dating back at least 2,500 years:

> "**Watch your thoughts,** for they become your words.
> **Watch your words,** for they become your actions.
> **Watch your actions,** for they become your habits.
> **Watch your habits,** for they become your character
> **Watch your character, for it becomes your destiny."**
> - *Frank Outlaw*

Keeping this quote close by our side, we can begin to understand the incredible power of our thoughts and how they ultimately shape our destiny. **The power of MONEYWINGS™ is knowing that you can choose your thoughts (the way you see money) and therefore guide your destiny, one brave feather a time!**

Here's another example from my life that illustrates the power of W.A.T.C.H.:

My higher beliefs about myself (*I am confident, independent, smart and strong*) got me through all the challenging patches in my life. Yet when it came to money, my limiting money-beliefs (*I am powerless, helpless, incompetent and fearful*) sat in the pilot seat, and kept my relationship to money and business success stalled on the ground.

It was no longer a mystery why I experienced constant "turbulence, flight delays and cancellations" in my entrepreneurial money dream, no matter what flight plan and preparations I designed for success. I *believed* I was powerless and therefore I *acted* powerless, and ultimately *created* powerlessness in my relationship to money. I believed money is something to fear, and therefore behaved with fear, and created even more fear in my relationship to money!

Becoming aware of your money beliefs that shape your financial perspective is an important beautiful, brave feather for your **MONEYWINGS™**.

It is no easy task shifting beliefs we feel are absolutely **true.** Human beings are not wired to change easily. Our primitive, critter brain acts up to keep us safe, even if that place is no longer good for us, and even when it's outright dangerous.

At the same time, evolutionary history shows time and time again that **those who are able to adapt and grow in spite of their fear (note - <u>not in absence of fear</u>) thrive.** Those who don't merely survive, without enjoying their right to experience life in all its glory.

Along my journey, I've learned that no matter who you are and how much or little income you earn, we ALL have a money story; we all carry varying amounts of money shame; and we all have self-limiting money beliefs. The good news is that as you grow your **MONEYWINGS™**

you get to shift your thoughts, take control of that pilot seat and move forward in your relationship with money.

So how can you start seeing money differently to support your money dream and attract success?

One of the biggest a-ha moments that first moved mountains in my business and relationship to money is when I discovered money is about so much more than just money!

In her beautiful book ***The Art of Money***, financial therapist Bari Tessler writes:

"Money isn't just about numbers; it's also about our relationship with *ourselves.* In order to shift our relationship with money, then we must untangle old patterns and challenge our assumptions about ourselves.... money always mirrors our inner world: the unresolved issues, suppressed gifts, and growing edges. So, when we get brave and bring love and mindfulness to our money relationship, it can become a sacred training ground where we unravel old knots, practice new skills, and learn to tango with these tender essential elements of life."

This exquisite, life-changing work continues to inspire and excite me with its endless possibilities for healing and prosperity in women's lives (men too!).

Chapter Three
Doubting It's Possible To Daring The Impossible

"There is freedom waiting for you on the breezes of the sky. And you ask, "What if I fall?" Oh, my darling, but what if you fly?"

- Erin Hanson

There's no doubt about it - stepping into a new experience in your relationship to money is brave stuff. Love takes courage, knowing your why, vision, having a supportive community, and lots of self-care. (Flowers, lovely scented candles, and nibbles of dark chocolate are wonderful too!). As Norman Vincent Peale wisely said, *nothing of great value in this life comes easily.*

Our brain is a meaning-making machine that forms our beliefs based on life experiences. It's important to understand this because we act on these beliefs as truth (whether they are true or not). For example, "I can only make good money working for someone else."

When we intentionally and mindfully take steps to create a new experience, we give our ourselves (our brain) the opportunity to see and create a new belief that's more closely in line with the truth. The truth sets us free -- this higher belief powerfully supports us to unfold our financial dream.

Not challenging our assumptions creates powerlessness to change, leaving us stuck in our self-limiting beliefs.

We then rob ourselves of our financial dream, deny ourselves our divine right to prosper, and remain in victim and survivor mode. We sit on the sidelines watching others unfold their financial potential while never experiencing our own financial success. Make sure assumptions and self- limiting beliefs aren't robbing you of the financial freedom you want. Challenging and questioning these beliefs can help you step more powerfully into the future you desire... rather than re- creating your past. One of the best gifts you can give yourself is being open and willing to change how you view money.

For me, seeing money differently began when I finally started to trust my intuition. Rather than pursuing the conventional route of learning the practical side of personal finance, I turned inward and asked myself the question, *how do money-smart people* think*? What do they see that I don't when it comes to money?*

To answer this question, I decided to read money quotes from financially successful people - over 850 in total - and gained a treasure-trove of wealth wisdom. In these quotes, I acquired the timeless, first steps for creating a healthy relationship with money. During my search for answers, I also discovered the entertaining and beloved classic parable, *The Richest Man In Babylon* (a story I plan to read together with my daughter).

On their own, these simple, rich books led me to a life-transforming discovery:

Money is never just about money.

This discovery empowered me to look at money differently. This new perspective freed me to re-shape my financial future and think big.

Linear thinking keeps you stuck in a job that you hate while creative, out-of-the-box thinking creates wealth. This non-linear way of thinking is what put me in the driver seat.

I soon found myself no longer thinking about problems but thinking about solutions to problems.

What's your money mindset? Do you think rich thoughts or poor thoughts?

In one of the best-selling personal finance books of all-time, *Rich Dad, Poor Dad*, author Robert Kiyosaki shares two different money mindsets between his own Dad ("poor dad") and his best-friend's Dad ("rich dad").

As Kiyosaki shares in ***Cashflow Quadrant***, his highly educated Dad strongly believed that "the love of money was evil and that excessive profit meant you were greedy... he was a good, honest, hardworking man who did his best to defend his point of view that money wasn't important to his life."

His "Rich Dad" saw money differently. In his view, money supports life. It's simply a tool that helps us live a fulfilled, happy life. "He thought it foolish to spend your life working for money and to pretend money wasn't important," Kiyosaki writes. "He believed that life is more important than money and that money is important for supporting life. He often said, 'You only have so many hours in a day, and you can only work so hard. So why work hard for money?'" Instead, his rich Dad made his money work for him by creating priorities and systems for saving and investing.

The identity of Kiyosaki's real rich dad was kept private due to a confidentiality agreement. Millions of people around the globe are impacted by the teachings of a man who never directly took the spotlight or credit for it.

On February 1, 2009, the Honolulu Advertiser published an obituary of a man named Richard Kimi, the real "rich dad" behind the book. When I saw his picture, I was a little surprised and delighted. I was expecting to see a dignified and stoic man clothed in a fancy, expensive suit and tie.

Instead, Kimi's celebration-of-life photo reveals a very casual sun-tanned, bare-chested man sitting at the edge of a swimming pool with his messy wet-hair toppled over his forehead, wearing a big, warm-hearted, down-to-earth twinkling smile. This is the photo that someone chose to capture who he was in life. A picture is worth a thousand words.

Bottom line, wealth is about our money mindset. How do you view money? You can either choose to have money and people work for you and be free to do the things that are important, or you can work hard for money.

Joseph Campbell, author of The Hero with A Thousand Faces" viewed money as "congealed energy" and believed that "releasing it releases life's possibilities."

Here are two examples of seeing money as energy:

In her book, *The Energy of Money*, author Maria Nemeth suggests doing the following exercise:

1. Take out a dollar bill. (Go ahead, pull a dollar out of your wallet, I'll wait. Got it?)
2. Hold it for a moment. Imagine everywhere this one-dollar bill has been, and everywhere it will be going. Think about the people who will hold it in the future, and what they will use it for.

Maria concludes that "the energy of this single dollar can flow from our hands into many people's lives."

In March 2017, one of the largest banks in South Africa, Ned Bank, re-positioned their branding to inspire clients *to see money differently* when they launched a beautiful 90-second video "Tale Of A Note" that frames the perspective of money as neither good or bad in itself, but reflects how we ourselves manage it (or mismanage it). A money maker narrates through the video and concludes: *Money is just paper. You have to admit... it's what you make of it."*

Belief-change work is powerful! There is more to cover on this subject than this brief chapter allows, but I want to leave you with some core steps for you to stop doubting and start daring to unfold your financial potential by stepping into a new experience that supports your financial dream.

My favorite teacher for this work is Elizabeth Purvis, creator of ***The Art of Feminine Magic***. Elizabeth affirmed what I was already doing right and empowered me with further support to help me create my financial dream. From her program, I learned that the quickest way to live my financial dream of raising a money-smart daughter is to **be the person who is already living that experience right now.**

How can we do this?

1. Know with clarity the financial dream you desire and want to create.
2. Identify the beliefs, actions and environment of the one who is living your financial dream.
3. Write a 1-sentence statement that captures how you see and experience yourself in this new way of being.
4. Create the experience of being the person you described in your statement.

External experiences powerfully shape us from the inside out. Consciously creating healthy experiences around money empowers you to shift your limiting money beliefs quickly and opens a whole new world of freedom for you to turn your financial dream into reality.

I grew up in a lower-middle class home in one of the wealthiest counties in the nation: Orange County, CA.

Later in college, the poster I hung in my college apartment revealed the money-beliefs I learned about what makes for a happy life. The poster was a picture of a large, perfect home overlooking a beautiful ocean sunset with 5 luxury cars parked below it. The title at the bottom read "Justification for Higher Education." The steady stream of consumer messages carried strong weight in those early days of my life, leaving me convinced it must be true: happiness lies in purchasing power and all it can buy. Of course, nothing could be further from the truth. **Money isn't about things, it's about people. Money is important, not because of things you can buy but because of the time and freedom it gives you to be with the people you love. It isn't money that makes you rich, it's the rich experience money gives you to be with those you care about.**

Several years ago, I re-wrote the lyrics to the song ***Looking For Love*** by Johnny Lee as a fun way to teach my daughter this valuable lesson:

Looking For Wealth In All the Right Places

Well, I spent a lifetime lookin' for you Credit cards and good-time spending left me blue
Playin' a fool's game, hopin' to win
And tellin' myself sweet lies at that dang ATM!

I was lookin' for wealth in all the wrong places Lookin' for wealth in too many Macy's Searchin' their aisles, lookin' for traces of what I'm dreamin' of Hopin' to friend a financial advisor

I'll bless the day I discover another heart, with lots of wealth.

Now that I found my own wings, I'm braver God bless the day I discovered you -oh you - (lookin' for wealth) in all the right places... (lookin' for wealth) inside, where the grace is.

Wealth is a beautiful thing. In the hands of a spiritual person, money becomes a powerful tool to contribute and shape the world around us. **The key is looking for wealth in all the right places, which is where wealth begins and ends -- in *you.***

Chapter Four
Discovering Wealth In Your Natural Gifts and Strengths

"You can only become truly accomplished at something you love. Don't make money your goal. Instead, pursue the things you love doing, and then do them so well that people can't take their eyes off you."

- Maya Angelou

I was no stranger to restaurant jobs. Paying my way through undergraduate work in college, I'd worked in several of them. However, it didn't take long to discover I made a terrible waitress.

All those important details that needed careful attention and execution, juggling multiple tables all at the same time, ensuring a great experience for the guest, simply did not match up to my natural strengths (whatever they were, I had no idea at the time) no matter how hard I tried.

I struggled miserably as a waitress but, in the process, I learned that I am a great hostess.

I thrived being the first point of contact, responsible for welcoming guests in preparation for their beautiful, delicious, fine-dining experience. In fact, the hardworking and savvy table-servers often shared their tips with me at the end of their shifts, letting me know how much they appreciated arriving at their tables with happy customers awaiting them.

I enjoy people and helping them feel welcomed. The problem was I earned more money as a waitress than a hostess. Sure, I could get the job done as a table server, but at great cost to my sanity, and budding self-confidence. I was never truly successful at it and the work left me unhappy.

While it deeply disappointed me, it didn't surprise me. "*Doing what you love won't earn you a good income... doing what you're good at doesn't matter, unless you're one of the "lucky few" who get that rare chance to follow your passion.* That was the message I heard growing up. My early work experience in the restaurant proved it true.

Brave-Heart Tip: When we believe something, our brain looks for evidence to support it.

Little did I know how very limiting this way of thinking truly was! These limiting beliefs became a pattern in my life preventing me from unfolding my financial potential.

You can be great at your gift, and learn how to monetize it, but if you carry the belief that it's not possible to make money doing what you love, it will never happen. As I shared in the last chapter, we create what we believe.

The internet has opened a whole new world for women to make money doing what they love, working smarter, not harder! I'm here to tell you that you CAN do what you love and make great money doing it.

Countless women entrepreneurs – many of them Moms – are making money online teaching what they're great at doing... marketing, writing, dating, parenting, spirituality, health and wellness, financial self-care and more.

I tell this story to share the passion in my heart for helping women transform their relationship to money by tapping into their natural talents and strengths.

It's the reason that I became a Certified Brain Personality Specialist and a Certified Money Coach.

Today, neuroscience shows tangible proof that we are born with natural talents and strengths to share in this world, intentionally and on purpose!

In fact, science proves the direct impact our thoughts have on the chemical balance in our brain which, in turn, affects our bodies. The fear and stress we hold around finances can cost us more than any amount of money we have in the bank.

It can cost us our precious health!

The first step to monetizing your gifts and strengths is learning what you're great at doing. Finding your natural zone of genius will empower you to travel from "here" to "there" towards your money dream.

It is a gift and responsibility to use our talents and lean into moving beyond our current financial challenges into a happier, healthier, more prosperous life.

One of the most powerful ways you can do this is to learn about your unique Brain Personality. Doing so can open your eyes to some of the greatest "a-ha!" moments, and provide you with an empowering, new perspective to authentically transform your life. As the great Albert Einstein reminded us, ***"You cannot solve a problem from the same consciousness that created it."***

To echo the words of my fabulous Brain Personality trainer Julie Anderson of Your Best Mind:

Your brain is your most important asset- more important than your house, your bank account, and stock portfolio.

I immediately fell in love with the knowledge Julie presented in her brain personality workshop. I promptly knew I had stumbled upon gold. The most common response I get from clients to whom I now teach this information to is *why wasn't I taught this in school? Everyone should know this stuff!*

Female brain-function experts such as Katherine Benziger, Arlene Taylor and Julie Anderson have taken research findings of well over a dozen neuroscience specialists and have organized the information into non-technical language to help us apply this knowledge into everyday life.

We can train our brains for success. Learning more about how our brain functions, communicates and processes information is essential in unfolding our incredible potential.

Ready for a quick peek into this amazing treasure within you? There is so much to share here, but as an introduction, I'm going to keep it very simple...

There are 5 components that make-up your *brain personality*:

- **Your Introversion / Extroversion Ratio.** The term Introvert and Extrovert have nothing to do with being shy or outspoken, timid or bold. This concept describes your brain's level of alertness. This portion of the brain sets the "volume control" in our life.

  An extrovert's brain requires greater amounts of stimulation than an introvert. An extrovert thrives in highly active environments. Extroverts need people interaction and naturally seek those opportunities regularly.

  Introverts, on the other hand, have a natural level of alertness and therefore require very little outside stimulus to keep engaged. Too much stimulus, in fact, can overload their brain. I love people, but as an introvert, being in big crowds too long can be draining for me. However, knowledge is power. Rather than avoid large events (as I had done in the past), I plan for them. Understanding these events will have a tendency to over stimulate, I deliberately schedule down time for a day or two afterwards to renew myself.

  When our environment matches our natural level of alertness, it sets the stage for our brain to function at its optimal level and helps us make the best use of our natural gifts and strengths, leading us to a happier, healthier life.

- **Your Brain Gender.** Although men and women complement each other well, there are chemical and structural differences in each brain, helping us to see that male and female brains *think*, *communicate*, and *process information* differently.

  Understanding these differences not only helps to improve communication and our relationships with each other, but also reveals specific strengths each genderhas to offer for creating personal success, as well as best outcomes for the greater good as a whole.

- **Your Communication / Sensory Preference Style**. This is also popularly known as our Learning Style. Our brain is naturally wired with a preference for how we process the information around us. Although we process information using all five of our senses (unless you suffered injury to any of them), our brain ordinarily processes information more effectively and efficiently through one style.

  The three sensory styles are Visual, Auditor and Kinesthetic (touch).

  Your Brain Lead (also known as Your Brain Quadrant Dominance):

Picture that your brain has four equal quadrants. These sections represent four distinct ways of our thinking style:

- the **Nurturer** specializes in harmony and connectedness, in tune with nature, loves animals and children, sentimental and sensitive, good Counselors, decorators, nurses.

- the **Master Coordinator** enjoys organizing, making lists, doing things "by the book", following rules in detail, repetitive and sequential tasks, dependable, practical, predictable, track time and money, bookkeepers, accountants, teachers.

-the **Innovator** thinks in pictures and symbols, highly intuitive, creative problem-solver, willing to take risks, entrepreneurial, loves change, sees new opportunities, visionary, sees things as they can be, not as they are, creative designers, consultants, architects, R&D.

-the **CEO/Boss** has written a life and business plan, logical, fact-based problem solver, enjoys being in charge and is good at it, enjoys using tools of all types, manages money well, careful spender, delegates authority well, makes decisions with ease, leaders of all types.

Brain researchers like Dr. Katherine Benzinger and Anne Sohn reveal that most of us are born with a biochemical bent towards *one* of these ways of thinking. A Master Coordinator who specializes in details would have done a far better job than I in my days as a waitress. As an Innovator, I struggle with details but easily see the big-picture, viewing life not as it is, but as it can be.

There is great power in understanding your thinking style, namely:

- being aware that there is a reason why you are healthier, happier and more successful when you operate inside your natural-born thinking style, whichever zone of genius it may be;
- knowing *why* you can do some activities all-day long without noticing time go by, while other tasks are terribly difficult for you to execute no matter what training, or salary increase you're given;
- being able to identify the reason why you may be feeling stuck;
- restoring harmony to relationships (including your relationship to money) at work and home by better understanding our spouse, children, supervisor and colleagues.

When putting this all together, it's incredibly important to remember that **none of the categories described within the five components above are better than another.** Introvert/Extrovert,Visual/Auditory/Kinesthetic, Nurturer/Innovator/Master Coordinator/Boss, Female/Male. Knowing our brain personality is marvelously VALUABLE to support not only our financial health, but our personal health as well, each personality special and precious in its own way.

It's also important to realize that **no two brains are the same.** Each of us is as unique as unique can be which helps me "keep calm and sparkle on" whenever sneaky, good-for- nothing comparison-itus attacks try snatching away the best me.

Brave-heart tip: We invite danger into our financial and personal well-being when we suppress our natural gifts.

Science proves that what we think directly affects the chemical balance in our brains, and in turn, affects our bodies. **You can never have too much happy!**

Take time to consider if you're living true to your gifts and strengths. If not, why? External expectations, limiting beliefs, labels, environment and even birth order can all play a role in preventing us from taking financial flight, even though we are born to fly.

I know many people struggle with negativity and never find their unique strengths because they either don't realize they have any, don't believe they are gifted or haven't attempted to discover their talents.

Helping people discover their gifts is the most life-giving part of my business. I know first-hand the transformative power it has to help women unfold their financial potential. I hope you have gained some powerful insights during this brief overview on a huge topic. I pray you feel inspired to learn more so that you can do more of what you love and get paid doing it. It's time to create your dream life and get busy sharing your gifts with the world.

Everybody has a gift - believe in your wonderfulness! I invite you to take a mini brain-personality quiz and discover your natural brain strengths today at my website www.brainhappylife.com.

Few things are as personally and financially rewarding than understanding your unique strengths, purpose and value in this life.

Chapter Five
Realizing Your Feminine Power To Prosper

"A wealthy woman is one rich in self-love.
Once you know your worth, you truly can have it all."

- @MindingHerBusiness

When my financial dream was born as a new mom to raise a money-smart daughter, I had no idea how to accomplish it. I did not in the least consider myself money-smart and my financial life reflected it. I dared to unfold my entrepreneurial wings but painfully struggled to get my business off the ground. Not even a $150 book on personal finance helped.

Although I didn't know it then, at the core of my dream was a quest to connect to my sense of value and self-worth. The possible death of my dream frequently loomed too close for comfort. Thankfully, I eventually followed my intuition and discovered how to see money differently and began the journey to heal my relationship to money.

I unfolded my financial dream to raise a money-smart girl while creating income doing what I love that honors my purpose, passion, values, gifts and strengths.

With this in mind, and as a creative mamapreneur, I run my life and business knowing with all my heart that the real journey to success is not about money.

It's about my joy of making a positive difference in a person's life, starting with my ability to show up as powerfully equipped as I can to do so.

Success certainly means different things to different people. John C. Maxwell beautifully and simply captures the way I view it. Mr. Maxwell defines success as "*knowing your purpose in life, growing to meet your maximum potential and sowing seeds that benefit others.*" How do you define success?

One of my favorite money stories is about a determined woman who turned her love for cookies into a $450 million- dollar empire. Of course, most of us would relish having such an extraordinary sum of money, especially doing what we love! Her financial success is awe- inspiring. Yet what deeply moves me beyond the money she created is the extraordinary *choice* Debbi Fields, founder of Mrs. Fields Cookies, made despite attempts of being shamed.

During dinner one night, at the beautiful, but intimidating home of one of her husband's clients, the man asked her "What do you do? "Oh," she replied, "I'm just trying to get orientated." The man got up, pulled an enormous leather-bound dictionary off the shelf, put it in her lap and said, "The word is *oriented.* If you can't speak the English language, you shouldn't speak at all." Incredibly embarrassed, Debbi Fields sat there in his library with tears streaming down her cheek. ("How Debbi Fields Built An Empire From Scratch", Libby Kane, LearnVest).

The man's shaming words and actions hurt terribly. In that moment, she could have let doubt reign and allow herself to remain feeling small and insignificant. Instead, she heard her father's voice who taught her **"that true wealth is found in family, friends and doing what you love."** That night, she gathered herself together and set out to live her purpose, grow to meet her maximum potential and sow seeds that benefit others. With the internal, emotionally healthy landscape she inherited from her family, she chose to love, trust her gifts and believe in herself. **The wealth she manifested on the outside reflected the wealth she already owned on the inside.**

In my own life, my grandmother has been a beautiful model of the feminine power to prosper. My daughter was born in a beautiful city with lots of rain. One day, my Mom bought a big-bright yellow plushy duck with a rain hat for our soon- to-be-born daughter. As a huge fan of Boston, and the book "*Make Way For Ducklings*", I fell in love with this darling duck. I later discovered that the duck had a button on its foot. When pressed, the duck moved from side to side, and sang: "singing in the rain! Just singing in the rain! What a glorious feeling, I'm happy again!" After my daughter was born, that duck eased her tears every time like magic.

It turns out that song "Singin' in the Rain" was a top hit in 1929 when another very special baby was born: my Grandma. The first generation in our family born in the United States, my grandma, the youngest of three sisters, was named Ernestina Gonzálcs. Her first year of life was during the great Depression of 1929, and yet like the song, she's always lived her life "singing in the rain", meaning that she's lived her life with a positive attitude, sense of purpose, and passion that gives her the courage to endure all kinds of stormy weather. My grandmother left elementary school to help support the family after her father endured a job-ending head-injury at work.

Later, she suddenly became a widow and a single-Mom at the age of thirty-five. Yet despite painful life events, she continually chose to celebrate life - with beauty, dance, song, laughter and above all a devotion to her family. She became a landowner in her 20's, owned all the cars she's ever driven, and owned all three houses she's ever lived in. She did all this while working in the same clothing factory for thirty- five years and taught herself how to manage the modest wages she earned.

But that's not all. **My grandmother's confident mindset, natural gifts and unique feminine strengths helped her create a happy life and financial security.** To this day, she often shares her favorite quote from Eleanor Roosevelt (who was 45 years old when my grandmother was born): **"Life is what you make it. Always has been. Always will be." You see, there is magic in choosing to sing in the rain!**

Today science reveals that men and women's brains are different, both structurally and biochemically which means we think, communicate and process information differently.

Marriage expert and comedian Mark Gungor's humorous *YouTube* video brings this reality to life in "The Nothing

Box." His entertaining presentation reveals men and women's different thinking styles and gives examples of how our brains sort things differently (The Nothing Box, You Tube Video by Mark Gungor).

As Dr. David Walsh of Mind-Positive Parenting so wisely shares: "there are significant differences (between the male and female brain) and simply ignoring them does a disservice to both sexes." One of my mentors and trainers in the field of brain-science, Julie Anderson, who is founder of Your Best Mind, points out that understanding the science behind how men and women's brains are wired differently "has a powerful implication for work, business and personal relationships!"

What they think about and focus on is different due to the size difference in certain brain areas. **Women are wired with a better "global view" of a life situation and can process information easier than men using both the right and left side of their brain. Because of this, they are better at long range planning. Men are better at the focused narrow view and short-range planning.** What a powerful combination when men and women join forces, working together to bring about successful outcomes in the home, at work, and in society.

A very special gift that women bring to any situation is their intuition. While many scoff at the idea of intuition, Julie Anderson (the brain expert I introduced you to in Chapter Four) goes on to explain that the study of the brain proves the existence of "intuition". Advanced brain imaging technology can now show the side of the brain that lights up when an individual is processing an intuitive thought or feeling.

The innovative side of our brain is naturally gifted at tapping into intuition. Earlier when I spoke about Brain Personality in Chapter Four, I talked about Innovators who have a natural brain dominance in the front, right Innovator quadrant of their brain. They tend to be naturally highly intuitive, whereas the brain uses more energy for the 75% others to access their intuition. Women tend to be more easily able to access their intuitive sense, especially women who are Innovators.

Brain science also reveals that women are natural-born leaders who are wired for success in the following ways:

- Women are opportunity experts. They tend to see opportunity in everything and everyone.

- We are experts at cultivating relationships, a vital skill for success especially in today's marketplace.

- Women are natural givers - an important quality in a healthy relationship to money. Most non- profits are run by female managers and volunteers.

- Women are excellent long-term strategic thinkers. We are more willing to rally behind a long-term, sustainable solution than a short-term fix.

So why don't we find more women leading with their natural-born talents? Great question! Here's what I have learned from my clients over the years. Simply put, women who aren't exercising their unique strengths and gifts often struggle with confidence.

As leadership guru Peter Drucker says, leadership is a state of mind. Remember those limiting beliefs I talked about in Chapter 2?

Leadership begins with embracing your natural gifts that leads to positive results and builds your self-esteem. When we change the way, we see ourselves in a more positive light, we begin to illuminate the world in more powerful ways.

"When you educate a man, you educate an individual. When you educate a woman, you educate a whole family."

- Robert Morrison McIver (1882- 1970), Scottish Sociologist and also an African proverb

Kayla Sloan is a freelance writer who covers business and personal finance. She has been featured in *The Huffington Post*, *Time*, *Entrepreneur Magazine* to name just a few. Kayla is passionate about helping people improve their finances so they can pursue their dreams with her blog at KaylaSloan.com. Kayla gives 8 reasons why women are successful in business:

- women ask for help
- women are persistent
- women know how to network and build relationships

- women are good communicators
- women are multi-taskers
- women are patient (as opposed to men's fight or flight stance)
- women's intuition
- women give credit when credit is due

And yet, women commonly struggle with under- earning. Despite our unique design for financial success, women earn less than men in today's marketplace. **While experts point to countless "barriers" to explain this income disparity, some of it is self-induced. Under-earners have several characteristics in common:**

- ***Under-earners undervalue their skills, talents and contributions.***

  Brave-Heart Tip: Standing in your power and owning your worth and talents may take practice, but the journey leads you closer to achieving your financial potential. Recognize the value you bring to the world and be ready to receive the income you deserve for your skills, services and/or products.

- ***Under-earners self-sabotage.***

  Brave-Heart Tip: Most of us are guilty of self-sabotage at one time or another in our lives. Some of the common ways that self-sabotage shows up in lives can include procrastination; giving up in the 11th hour of our miracle; spending too much time "dreaming" and not enough "doing"; neglecting our self-care; being unforgiving when mistakes are made; not showing up; allowing negative people to zap our energy, enthusiasm and confidence; and more. Equally important to understanding how we sabotage our success, is the need to understand why. Listen to your self-talk, recognize self-sabotaging thoughts or habits, notice and honor what you need to get back on track, and gently focus back on what you set out to accomplish.

- ***Under-earners fly under the radar.***

  Brave-Heart-Tip: Successful people stretch beyond their comfort zone; they regularly take risks instead of always playing it safe. Believing in ourselves is a muscle we can practice by acknowledging and reassuring our fears instead of allowing them to dictate our choices. Risks can seem much bigger in our minds than they actually are. Practice courage stepping beyond your comfort zone, one brave feather at a time.

Change begins with choice. It begins with you. You are your own financial savior, with the beautiful creative power to change your destiny and seize the success you deserve. It all begins with saying "yes". Yes, to your financial dream, which is the key to your financial breakthrough. I encourage you to create a list of what is stopping you from allowing your financial success to unfold. Some examples women have shared with me are:

- Fear
- Lack a support system to help them on their path
- Relying on someone or some circumstance to save them.
- Relying on someone to figure things out for them.
- Their financial dream is not aligned with their values, strengths, skills or passion.

They've forgotten who they are along the way by putting everyone else's needs first before their own. Do any of these resonate with you? Or perhaps there is another reason that more closely describes your challenge? The important thing is to be honest with yourself and write it down. Awareness creates a new way of seeing yourself and reveals opportunities once hidden from sight. It allows you to discover new solutions to old problems, and experience freedom to redefine yourself as often as you desire.

When you are ready, go a step further, and identify the choices you've made in relation to that challenge. Gently and bravely take ownership of those choices, remembering you are not alone!

Together, when we take responsibility for our financial life

-- with compassion, forgiveness and determination -- we give ourselves the power to transform our financial circumstances and positively impact those around us.

Now is the time to embrace your unique value and gifts that you have been given to experience the prosperity, peace and joy that you deserve. Now is the time to love more and fear less, as you unfold your feminine power to prosper.

Chapter Six
LET'S GET TENDER™

Re-Writing The Stars Of Your Money Story

"Where your treasure is, there will your heart be also."

- JK Rowling, Harry Potter and the Deathly Hallows / Matthew 6:21

I didn't know anything about limiting beliefs when I was 28, but I remember shaking my head feeling confused by the religious center's rule that day.

Cheerfully walking into their office one morning, I inquired about enrolling in their training program to become a Spiritual Director. It took me a moment to register the kind secretary's reply: "*I'm sorry. You're too young.*"

From life experience and inside my heart, I could see that the rule reflected an underlying message of limited faith rather than unlimited possibilities.

In my imaginative fashion, I respectfully asked if they would consider making an exception? After all, I was a religious education grad student at the time, enrolled in a well- respected Catholic college. I had not only experienced a few years of spiritual direction myself, but already had one year of spiritual direction training under my belt from a distinguished facility across the country, the Mercy Center in Burlingame, CA.

However, I learned that I was not even close to the qualifying age for the program. The secretary gently explained I could apply on my 35th birthday after I gained more life experience for the work. (As it turned out, when I was finally old enough to apply, the center no longer existed.)

Leaving disappointed but mostly confused, I knew the rule didn't fit the reality of my experience. From a relatively young age, I felt drawn to spirituality that began in my late teens. I ultimately followed a path into professional pastoral church ministry, retreat work and co-hosting a Catholic TV program aired on TBN, the largest Christian broadcast network in the world (and Armed Forces Network) into 110 million homes across the country.

Perhaps the secretary was right about one thing: Without the wisdom I have today, I accepted rather than questioned the rule. In hindsight, I would have suggested that 20-year- olds in the college town might have benefitted from the option to do spiritual direction with someone closer to their own age.

The rules we live by are worth examining. This is especially important when it comes to our money beliefs and rewriting the stars of our money story.

You'll recall that I briefly introduced limiting money beliefs in Chapter 1. A limiting money-belief is something you believe to be true about money, or about your relationship to money, which holds you back from unfolding your authentic, untapped, financial potential.

These beliefs may keep you blind to opportunities and prevent you from sharing your natural strengths and talents. They often keep you stuck and prevent you from achieving your financial dreams no matter how hard you try.

There are many different types of self-limiting money beliefs. Here are some common ones (but there are as many as there are unique individuals in the world):

"It's not safe to have money." "Money is the root of all evil." "It's not spiritual to have money."

"You have to work hard for money." "Rich people are greedy and dishonest." "There's a limit to how much I can earn."

"I can only make good money working for someone else."

"I have enough to get by."

"It's too difficult to get out of debt."

"If I make more money than my family, they won't love me."

Do you recognize any of these beliefs in your money story?

Through belief-change work, I discovered my greatest limiting belief that prevented me from unfolding my financial potential:

I believed I could not be spiritual and wealthy. In my mind, a clear un-crossable boundary existed between faith and finances.

As a result, I felt doomed to financial hardship since my greatest gift is faith - a spiritual perspective that empowers others to see beyond what's visible to what's possible.

Becoming aware of a self- limiting belief is the first step that gives you the power to change it.

At first, I played around with this belief by reframing it into an opposite statement: I can be spiritual and wealthy. When I first "tried it on to see how it fit", it felt very uncomfortable and even scandalous to think such a thought. *Impossible! Rubbish!* I thought. Still, my mind searched for evidence beyond me, and the possibility awakened that maybe it could be true.

I considered multi-billionaire Bill Gates. I thought of his wealth and the powerful resources he had to contribute to his philanthropic work overseas. In his words, his focus for money had changed to "getting the resources out to the poorest in the world."

I also thought of billionaire Oprah Winfrey, a spiritual woman with tremendous wealth who shares her wealth in abundantly creative ways such as her leadership academy for girls in South Africa.

Like many women I know, I am a giver. It would be a financial dream to have enough wealth to take care of my family and also help heal the planet through philanthropic means.

There is a saying that money is neither good nor bad. It simply reveals our character. The high character revealed in both of these wealthy individuals created the first crack in my assumption that wealth and spirituality do not mix.

When I shifted into believing that I can be spiritual and wealthy, a whole new world opened up for me. I continually reflected on this new belief within the context of my background as a spiritual teacher, and all I was learning to heal my relationship to money as a female entrepreneur. It dawned on me that it would be wonderful to bring both worlds together and call it *financial spirituality*. Did such a concept even exist, I wondered?

To my utter-delight, a fateful Google search led me to discover a beautiful little book published in 2007 - the year my daughter was born - titled *Financial Spirituality*!

As a financial advisor who has served as a pastor, author Bill Rowland has a unique perspective on spirituality and finance. His innovative book is filled with new ways of looking at old problems.

His graceful, down-to-earth, compassionate teaching style fluidly bridges money and spirituality with practical applications. It is a fundamental resource I've implemented into my heart-centered money coaching practice for money healing and basic money practices.

Above all, his financial and spiritual perspective finally helped me to get very clear and understand without a doubt that the truth is - you can be spiritual and wealthy if you so choose to be.

"At first people refuse to believe that a strange new thing can be done, then they begin to hope it can be done, then they see it can be done – then it is done and all the world wonders why it was not done centuries before."

– Frances Hodgson Burnett, 19th century American writer

I can still remember the short-and-sweet sentence I read in the first few pages of my Personal Finance book and the great relief it gave me: **Personal finance is not rocket science.**

In the same way, reading Bill's sentence a few years later felt like incredibly sweet music to my ears: **At their core, finances are a spiritual matter.**

This is the heart of **MONEYWINGS™** and my podcast **Let's Get Tender™: Money Conversations that Matter.** (Tender refers to a woman's spiritual unfolding of her financial potential as well as *legal* tender, also known as money). As author Bill Rowland points out, "finances begin at a very deep place."

I take my clients through the process of rebuilding a financial belief system that works for them - one that helps them make better decisions, take action and follow through. Everything starts to make sense (and cents) as their relationship to money becomes deeply meaningful beyond the physical dollars and cents. This often-misunderstood area of our life can finally get the attention it deserves.

Here are seven spiritual wisdom lessons I've learned and share in my financial spirituality workshops to help women start re-writing the stars of their money story:

Lesson #1: You Are The Average of the Five People You Spend Time With

Be mindful of these spiritual resources in your life as you shift into new money habits that support your financial dream. Keep closest to you those who add to your spiritual energy reserves. Be aware of those who draw energy away from you. How you manage your energy is so important. Practice healthy boundaries. Learn the elegant art of saying "no."

Give yourself permission to be more than you imagined possible. Believe in yourself!

Lesson #2: Your Unique Gifts Are A Spiritual Resource

I shared much about this in Chapter 4. However, it is important to understand that whatever your unique gift is (knowledge, experiences, connections, intuition, understandings, talent, skill...) it is a spiritual resource. Like any spiritual resource, it must be shared. Hidden away it disappears, but shared it grows.

Lesson #3: Forgive and Let Go of Money Shame

One of my favorite teachers for money healing is Bari Tessler Linden, author and founder of *The Art of Money.* Money shame is such a big, tender, deep part of money work in financial spirituality.

In this short space, let it suffice for now as gentle, loving encouragement:

Be at peace knowing you are taking action now (*in just reading this book!*) **to change things.**

Lesson #4: Move Forward With Mini Baby Steps One Brave Feather At A Time Remember the story of the Tortoise and the Hare? **Slow and steady.** Instead of racing to achieve the change you seek, focus all your attention on the next mini-action step again and again and again. My daughter learned this lesson in kindergarten. Racing to finish her dreaded writing assignment only dragged out the process even longer. That's when she learned that "fast is slow and slow is fast." Consistency is key for transformation. It creates momentum; builds self-confidence; positively shapes your self-identity as new beliefs replace old beliefs that no longer serve you; and thus empowers you to be the change you seek. One brave feather at a time glides you safely into the finish line.

Lesson #5: Automate New Money Habits

Over the past 3 years, automation has become a powerful tool I use in my personal finances and in my coaching business that allows money to flow more easily into my life. It can do the same for you. Set yourself up for success! Put systems in place (manual or virtual) that will allow you to complete money tasks in an automatic way so that habits for improvement settle in more easily into your new way of doing things. This may take a little research, planning and experimenting but it is a money-smart way of managing your spiritual energy around change.

Lesson #6: Believe There Is Abundance All Around You

One of the thoughts that held me back from helping more women and creating more income was the belief that there was **not enough of me to go around**. I wondered how successful women could lead such large communities without burning out? This belief kept me stuck for a long time. The truth is, fear can lead to tunnel vision. A powerful tool for overcoming fear and tunnel vision is **imagination.** Reframing my belief ("there is enough of me to go around") fired up my imagination to see things differently and to creatively find at least three ways to make it true.

For example, I could outsource work, upgrade my self-care habits, set healthy boundaries, ask for help, build a team around me to support my success and more. From a spiritual perspective, resources remain hidden from us *when we don't believe they're there.* Yes, faith and imagination magically open our eyes to the abundance all around us. A great example is a classic, childhood-favorite story of mine, Stone Soup (see "Recommended Resources" at the back of the book).

Lesson #7: Transform Limiting Beliefs Into Empowering Beliefs That Positively Energize Your Financial Dream

Here are the five steps I've discovered that can help you start to question your limiting beliefs and ultimately free you from them:

- Ask if the belief is true... and really listen to the answer.
- Write the opposite statement. (e.g., making money is easy vs. making money is hard)
- What evidence can you find that supports this new truth?
- Notice how you feel when you believe this new truth (stress? peace? free?)
- Claim this new "un-limiting" belief and live in this new truth.

It's exciting to witness so many heart-centered women beginning to re-write their money stories, step into their financial potential and powerfully share the goodness they are meant to share in the world, as they overcome their self- limiting money beliefs.

Which lesson above speaks most to you to support you in unfolding your financial dream? What limiting belief are you willing to let go? What new truth are you open to receiving in support of your financial dream?

Along the way, you may discover as I did, that money ultimately connects us to one another and to the world around us. The experience of having money brings a deep sense of financial security, trust and freedom to enjoy life. At its core, money is a spiritual matter ultimately reminding us that we are all connected and we are never, ever alone.

Chapter Seven
Growing MONEYWINGS: Setting Course For Your Financial Dream

"How do I let go?" she asked. The teacher smiled and said, "Reach for something you desire more."

- Lisa Schrader

If you've arrived to this page... yay You! Congratulations! I believe that if this book has found its way into your hands, **it's for a reason.** The concepts, strategies and tools that you've been shown have the power to transform your financial life.

You have accomplished an amazing feat that most people never experience - seeing money through fresh eyes! That's because we tend to surround ourselves with information that matches our beliefs, but we do so at the risk of ignoring or dismissing another perspective that might actually be closer to the truth that sets us free.

During graduate school, I personally experienced a powerful example of this. I've always loved dance but never took it seriously as a career path or even pursued it as a hobby. During my studies at Boston College, however,

I had the opportunity to stretch beyond my comfort zone and enrolled in an elective Liturgical Dance class.

Although I felt completely like a fish out of water, I relished the experience of learning body movements to spiritual music. One of our assignments was to choreograph our own movements to a musical arrangement. I was not surprised that I found the homework easy to complete and performed it fairly confidently the next day in class. What did surprise me is what happened next.

During the final class, our professor displayed a video-taped presentation of our individual, choreographed performances. After watching several students perform their pieces, a dancer appeared on the screen that I did not recognize. She was such a natural, so graceful and beautiful, I didn't remember seeing her in class. I asked, "Who's that?" The students and professor quickly replied, "That's you Marlene!" It was obvious to everyone who had seen that dancer, except to me.

For several seconds, I sat there stunned (and slightly embarrassed for not recognizing my own self). I simply could not believe it was *me*. For one brief moment in time, I felt like a stranger to myself, completely disconnected from ever realizing that potential lived within me... until I saw myself through a fresh perspective. It's time to see your relationship with money through fresh eyes! You've come this far... let's keep your **MONEYWINGS™** growing!

Believe in your brave heart and blazing imagination to thrive! Here are eight money mindsets to carry in your purse and in your heart:

1. **We create what we <u>BELIEVE</u>.** One of the most successful women I heard speak gave a lesson full of key points. At the end of her talk, each point led to her core message: "*If you believe, you will succeed.*" Janice Bryant Howroyd is the 1st African American to lead a billion- dollar business.

2. **90% of success is <u>IN</u> how you show up.** Be ever-mindful of your thoughts, words, actions and habits for they lead to your character and destiny. Create an environment around you that supports your success including your physical space, mindset, routines, and the people you allow (and don't allow) into your space. Surround yourself with those who believe in you and energize you to blossom. Sit in the driver's seat - take full responsibility for your life and well-being.

3. **Live in YOUR full potential to shine.** Avoid "comparison-itis". The illusion I followed trying to be like everyone else only lead me in circles! Move forward instead, pouring your energy and focus into being someone you love. Know your purpose, your clear desired outcome and daily inspired actions to achieve it. Be the honest channel you can only be, and then allow the Universe to take care of the rest. *You'll be astounded at the miracles you'll experience!*

4. **Be <u>BRAVE</u>**. Self-limiting money beliefs are like sticky goblins --they become so much a part of you,

you don't even realize they're there. When you're stuck in frustration, unable to move past your fears and feel tempted to settle, remember that you are closer to your goal than you think!

Rest and then ask yourself, "what if..." to shift your perspective. One of the bravest questions I asked is *what if I can be spiritual* and *wealthy?* The truth set me free. "Friend" courage.

5. **The <u>HEART</u> of financial success lies in relationships.** *I cannot emphasize this enough: Know your value and self- worth.* Honor your feminine leader qualities to create, nurture and transform! Women are especially gifted in building relationships. You are empowered to generate amazing income and impact in the world. Know that you already have *everything* to begin and you'll experience financial freedom quicker than you can imagine.

6. **You <u>AND</u> I cannot accomplish great things alone.** We need others to achieve the greatness we were born to share. Brain science reveals the valuable ways we need a support team to shine in our full potential as individuals and as a society. The beauty of "left brain", "right brain", male and female teams working together is essential for creating unlimited possibilities to thrive.

7. **Honor your <u>BLAZING</u> zone of genius.** Everybody has a gift - trust yours. I've always seen the world through eyes of faith and innovation, but greatly undervalued these strengths based on the opinions of others. As a result, my world became

very small and financially unstable. When I learned to be vulnerable in safe places to connect with others, opportunities "magically" appeared. Live in your unique design and you'll soon ignite a flourishing, joyful life.

8. **Value the world of pure <u>IMAGINATION</u>.** Guard your freedom to view life not only as it is, but as it could be. When you struggle trying to figure out "the how" of a situation, remember Einstein who said, "We cannot solve problems with the same thinking we used when we created them." Focus on the outcome you wish to achieve, and "the how" will present itself to you.

I encourage you to re-read MONEYWINGS™ and take the time to pause and reflect on sections that are most meaningful to you at this time so you can put your mind, heart and soul into taking baby steps forward.

Setting the course for your financial happy-ever-after begins with your decision to make it happen and creating a financial belief-system and financial self-care practice that supports your dream. **A simple 3-step plan of action that you can easily remember for growing MONEYWINGS™ are these three simple words: TALK- LEARN- GROW.**

Talk about money, learn about money and grow in your relationship to money. Find an accountability buddy. Read money books (I've listed some recommendations for you in the Resources section). Choose one limiting money belief to work on for a week, a month, a season or a year.

Set yourself up for success by following one or two strategies in this book. Consider working privately with a money coach or join a group coaching program.

The benefits you can expect from stepping into this work of healing your relationship to money are bountiful. Here are some of the benefits you can expect:

- Peace of mind around your finances.
- Connecting more deeply to your value and self-worth.
- Understanding your money story, patterns, habits, beliefs (why you do what you do when it comes to your finances).
- Easier conversations with your spouse/family about money and personal finances.
- Understanding the language and energy of money.
- Confidence in your power to unfold your financial potential.
- Ability to set boundaries that support your financial dreams, goals and potential.
- Awareness of self-limiting subconscious money-beliefs and patterns.
- A meaningful relationship to money based on your strengths, desires, values and priorities.
- Above all, knowledge that you are no longer walking alone on your journey to your financial dream.

Here's a secret that every successful person already knows. Don't wait for something to happen. Make it happen. If any of the lessons in this book resonated with you, take action now, don't wait. Really, don't wait! Transformation takes *time.* My biggest piece of advice for you is don't wait to unfold your financial dream. As Mel Robbins explains in The 5 Second Rule, "*If you have an impulse to act on a goal, you must physically move within five-seconds or your brain will kill the idea.*"

Don't let this opportunity slip through your fingers. Find one action you can take in the next five seconds to begin unfolding your financial dream. You will find that once you have accomplished your first goal, each subsequent goal will get easier.

Knowing *what to do* is not enough to achieve your financial dream. Knowing *why you need to do it* will also never be enough. Whatever you feel moved to do, you need to show yourself (your brain) that you are serious by taking some form of action, no matter how small or simple it might be.

The fact that you took time to read this book tells me that you are ready to invest in yourself which makes me even more excited to see how taking action one brave feather at a time changes your financial life.

In fact, I have a confession...

I think of my daughter and you dear reader as I dance around the house with the volume turned up anytime I hear "Re- Write The Stars" (from the movie-musical hit, *The Greatest Showman*). As a money coach, I love this song and video for so many reasons: The beautiful harmonies, stunning in-air choreography, lovely vision of masculine-feminine energy intertwined -- *but especially the words.* From a financial perspective, the words so powerfully capture the dynamic dance of daring to rewrite the stars of our money story with all our dreams, doubts, hopes, challenges and courage.

In fact, you may ask, "*Is it possible?*" Yes! It's up to you. No one can say what you get to be. So how can you re- write the stars of your money story?

With MONEYWINGS™ ...one brave feather at time.

In Closing

"Sometimes your only available transportation is a leap of faith."

- Margaret Shepard

Dear beautiful reader, thank you for taking this journey to learn how to unfold your financial potential. I hope this book has touched your heart, encouraging and inspiring you to start living your financial happy-ever-after. I am so very grateful to you for taking the time to read it, and even maybe sharing it as a gift for someone you care about who is struggling with money challenges. It's a tender and exciting moment when you realize that you get to design and create your own financial dream.

It leads you to the daring question that only you can decide:

Will you choose to do so?

Here's the great news!

The moment you realize that financial power is about the choices you make, you start growing **MONEYWINGS™**.

The moment you see that your financial power is not inside your bank account (or in any material possession you may or may not own) but already lies within you, it unlocks your freedom to soar.

Every conscious, brave choice you make to transform your financial dream into reality adds a beautiful new feather to your financial wings.

It's as simple as that.

The money story you've lived in the past to this point does not matter *except* for the richest, most valuable lessons you choose to employ for your next financial steps today, tomorrow and in the future.

What matters most is what you choose to do next.

Here's what I recommend:

Choose to move forward into your financial future, grateful for every lesson that life has taught you thus far about your relationship to money - the good, the bad and the ugly.

Choose to pick yourself up, dust your feet off, and focus on the beautiful financial dream that your heart is calling you to create for you and your family.

Choose to love yourself enough to live the financial reality you deserve.

There's no better time than right here, right now to choose, once and for all, to grow your **MONEYWINGS™**.

It's a very intimate journey - I get it. It can feel impossible to breakthrough money challenges. You may feel tempted to give up a thousand times! Remember your compelling "why" behind your financial dream. Pick one of the tools or strategies in this book and get started. Time is precious. Don't wait. Transformation takes time. I promise if you stick with it, you'll learn that you *can* do it.... and that changes everything! It's an incredible feeling when you finally breakthrough your roadblocks to reach the other side where your dream lies. It's an experience that no one can create for you.

An amusing image I often use during my workshop to illustrate **MONEYWINGS™** is a cartoon of two little birds sitting high atop a branch. One of them worrisomely peers straight down at the ground with a parachute securely tied to her back. The other bird perched natural and free, looks at her anxious friend and casually says, "*maybe we should try jumping without the parachute this time.*"

Even with every bit of preparation, you may never truly feel ready to leap, but I'm here to gently and positively remind you that *you are equipped to fly and soar!*

There's no doubt about it - growing **MONEYWINGS™** requires as much courage, laughter, compassion and gentle self-care that you can muster.

MONEYWINGS™ is my love note to help you reclaim and restore your confidence back to where it belongs. Wings protect, guide, lift, and break. They are as tender as they are powerful... just like you and me.

When my relationship to money was broken, I always felt the need to be perfect in every little thing. But as I gained financial health and strength, my heart only cared to soar -- even with a broken wing.

It's not about being perfect.

It's about staying true to yourself, listening to your heart, and letting love, not fear, lead the way.

Your money story is sacred ground containing the very richest soil to cultivate a beautiful, meaningful and prosperous life.

I hope this book has supported and inspired you to choose to unfold your beautiful **MONEYWINGS™,** one brave feather at a time. May you SOAR!

Bonus Chapter
Entrepreneurship: Monetizing Your Natural Gifts

"Life is about moments:
The moment you find your passion, the moment you decide to follow it and the moment you realize you can actually make money doing it."

-Codie Sanchez, Investor, Entrepreneur, Advocate, Speaker

Welcome to the world of female entrepreneurship! Positivity. Determination. Confidence. Organization. Knowing Your Strengths. Personal Growth. Gratitude. Support System. Self-Control. Planner. Game-Changer.

Entrepreneurship isn't for everyone. But if you have an inkling of interest in the subject, or a sneaking suspicion that you just might be an entrepreneur-at-heart, then grab a cuppa Joe and lean in.... this bonus chapter is for you!

My journey as an entrepreneur began seven years ago when I took my four-year-old daughter to a craft faire. Just before we exited the show, my eyes spotted some sparkling high- end jewelry. I didn't even wear jewelry, but it was so beautiful, I explained to my little-one, "*Mommy is just going to take a quick peek*." Seeing the jewelry up close, I discovered the brand name looked so familiar, but I couldn't place where I'd seen the name before. To this day, it remains a mystery to me.

I learned that the Founder of the jewelry business had a dream that echoed my own: *To have a business that would allow her to be at home with her children.* She realized that selling jewelry could empower other women to build a business of their own. An hour later after my preschooler finally succeeded in tugging me away, I had happily invested in starting my own business as a jewelry consultant. Within three months, I'd built a team of five women to join me in a jewelry-world of business that recorded over $125 million and over 40,000 consultants nation-wide.

When I started in business, entrepreneurship just felt like the right fit for me. I followed my instinct and trusted myself enough to take a leap of faith into work that gives me tremendous joy, regardless of the challenges and hard work of walking the road less traveled.

Several years later, when I learned my brain is indeed naturally wired as an Innovator for entrepreneurship, the scales fell from my eyes revealing powerful confirmation that I was right on track where I was meant to be! It explained why I always felt miserable and lost working 9-5 jobs and terribly misunderstood when others couldn't understand why I'd risk leaving a steady paycheck with benefits. Frankly, I wondered what was wrong with me too! Yet *deep* in my heart, anything less than running my own business gave me that awful feeling of *settling* - something Innovators are not built to do at all, as you'll read below. Understanding my unique gifts powerfully equipped me to maximize my efforts to financially succeed as an entrepreneur.

Back in Chapter Four where I shared more on this topic, you can find a link to complete a mini-Brain Personality Quiz so you too, can discover your beautiful strengths for work and life.

When I started in business, I also didn't understand that there is a difference between an entrepreneur and a small business owner.

An entrepreneur is a dreamer and takes much bigger risks than a small business owner. **Entrepreneurs are never satisfied with the status quo. We are always thinking of the next big project. We feel a constant urge for growth and progress.** Small business owners concentrate on one thing at a time, avoid failure and hate to lose. They do not juggle things like entrepreneurs do. They prefer to know what they are having for lunch three days in advance as opposed to entrepreneurs who can thrive in chaos. Entrepreneurs are out to change the world! Small business owners are more interested in profit margins, revenue projections and support costs. Entrepreneurs love what they do. Small business owners don't necessarily love what they do but are happy doing it because it means they get to be their own boss with more control over their work and family life.

Do you recognize any of these traits? *Is there an entrepreneurial spirit in you longing to be free?*

Neither is better than the other... small business owners and entrepreneurs can learn much from each other in the different ways they run their companies.

Learning the differences between how an entrepreneur and small business owner think empowered me to gain clarity and step more confidently forward in my business as an entrepreneur. It awakened in me the exciting realization that we as women are naturally gifted for entrepreneurship (as share more about in Chapter Five). This knowledge freed me to make money a priority for my business, guilt- free, and helped me to identify the areas I needed to improve and develop for success.

I'll never forget the simple, yet-not-so-simple advice my business coach gave me during our first session together. **You are in business for one reason, and one reason alone to make money. Without money, there is no business.** As a creative entrepreneur, who happens to be a money coach, I really appreciated his advice and understood what he meant.

In the big picture, the business exists as a system for monetary exchange for a valuable service purchased by a client - customer. With this perspective in mind, I knew it was essential to build healthy business finance practices such as keeping an eye on profit margins, keeping costs low and margins high, measuring ROI (return on investment), checking for improper credit control, and on and on and on.

And yet at the same time, business is done not with money, but with people. That's why I often say that money isn't about paper. It's about people.

Andy Warhol captures this dance of money for entrepreneurs, who unlike small business owners, are not focused on the money but on the greater good the business serves:

"Being good in business is the most fascinating kind of art. Making money is art and working is art and good business is the best art."

- Andy Warhol Entrepreneurship *is* an art. It calls us into our personal relationship to money and mindful business practices to serve our dear clients / customers at the highest level of service possible. This is why financial spirituality is so important as a female entrepreneur.

The following list offers a quick peek into what prevents entrepreneurs from successfully unfolding their financial dream:

- An inability or unwillingness to take risks
- The time and effort it requires
- Difficulty attracting capital (money) for their project
- Lack of business management skills
- Lack the "know-how" for starting a business
- Lack knowledge about their market and industry
- Family/financial pressures to keep a traditional, steady job.

Did you notice the common denominator that lies at the heart of all but one of these challenges? Every perceived obstacle on the list is a result of an inner personal choice, rather than an outside entity preventing the individual from success.

The truth is that if you are a new or aspiring female entrepreneur, you can do it if you make the choice to do so! You have more opportunity to succeed than you realize. It all starts with your power to say yes to your destiny.

I understand the courage it requires to take a leap of faith. However, I also know the exciting rewards that come with it.

You and I have the same hours in a day as any highly successful entrepreneur. There is no better time than the present to begin your entrepreneurial journey. Opportunities abound! The support for women entrepreneurs is growing where more women and men are stepping up to help fund female entrepreneurs. There are a multitude of wonderful business coaches teaching women how to work smarter, not harder; how to manage their time; how to start a business and understand the "ins and outs" of business.

Entrepreneurship is the dance of being a dreamer, thinker, storyteller and leader. Entrepreneurs are the dreamers who create the vision; the thinker who formulates all the details in a business plan; the storyteller who speaks and sings the dream; and the leader who coordinates it all to move the project forward.

I want women entrepreneurs to know that **MONEYWINGS™** is an identity every woman can embrace as a safe-harbor to journey into her financial dream.

From the moment I discovered the gorgeous, ground-breaking world of online entrepreneurship, I knew in my heart it was the place for me. Thanks to the internet and many useful tools, it's now possible for women around the world, especially those with children, to start businesses and earn money from home. Whether providing a little-extra income for the family, or seeking to earn a full-time income, online entrepreneurship is one of the most exciting places where women are experiencing endless opportunities to create money doing what they love with more influence and impact than ever before!

After swimming in these waters daily as a women's coach for the past 3 years, the three most valuable secrets I wish I knew when I first started, that every new or aspiring entrepreneur needs to know are these:

There is a right way and a wrong way to start an online business. This one piece of advice alone will not only save you tons of precious time and money, it beautifully and powerfully positions you for success right from the start (which is the least you deserve for the faith and courage it takes to bloom and shine as an entrepreneur!).

There is a learning curve -- expect and plan for it. The most successful businesses can make online entrepreneurship look easy, but the truth is learning how to make money online is an art that takes time and practice. You can learn the system. It requires a spirit of patience and celebration that you're daring to grow beyond your comfort zone, rather than frustration and comparison-itis that too often leads women to give-up just before their business would have taken flight.

Success requires support. After lesson #1 and #2, this secret can be the most challenging for strong, self-reliant independent women like you and me to accept. This has been one of the most rewarding benefits I did not expect to experience when I first set out on my entrepreneurial adventure. Unfolding my financial potential required me to allow myself the gift of being supported and became the greatest secret behind strengthening my wings to truly fly. I highly recommend seeking 1 x 1 private mentorship over group coaching (if at all possible). I learned the hard way that I would have spent less money and time in the long-run, with faster results, doing this from the start.

The benefits and rewards of female entrepreneurship far outweigh the challenges. There has never been a better time for women to start their own businesses than now! :)

Recommended Resources

BOOKS: ON MONEY

"The Richest Man in Babylon." By George Samuel Clason, New York: Penguin Random House, 2002.

" ***The Seven Stages of Money Maturity: Understanding the Spirit and Value of Money in Your Life."*** By George Kinder. New York: Dell, 1999.

"Breaking Money Silence: How To Shatter Money Taboos, Talk More Openly about Finances, and Live A Richer Life." By Kathleen Burns Kingsbury. Santa Barbara, CA: Praeger, 2017.

"The Opposite of Spoiled: Raising Kids Who Are Grounded, Generous, and Smart About Money." By Ron Lieber. New York: Harper Collins, 2016.

"The Energy of Money: A Spiritual Guide to Financial and Personal Fulfillment." By Maria Nemeth. New York: Ballantine, 1999.

"Money Magic: Unleashing Your True Potential for Prosperity and Fulfillment." By Deborah L. Price.

Novato, CA: New World Library, 2000.

"Your Money or Your Life: 9 Steps to Transforming Your Relationship with Money and Achieving Financial

Independence." By Robin Vicki and Joseph R. Dominguez. New York: Penguin Books, 2008.

"Financial Spirituality." By Bill Rowland. MI: BookSurge, 2007.

"Overcoming Underearning: Overcome Your Money Fears and Earn What You Deserve." By Barbara Stanny. New York: HarperCollins, 2005.

"The Art of Money: A Life-Changing Guide To Financial Happiness." By Bari Tessler. Berkeley, CA: Parallax Press, 2016.

ON FEMALE ENTREPRENEURSHIP

"Your Business Sweet Spot. Simplify Your Business, Amplify Your Results." By Racheal Cook. Richmond, VA: The Yogipreneur, 2016.

"Self-Made: Becoming Empowered, Self-Reliant, and Rich in Every Way." By Nely Galan. New York: Speigel and Grau, 2016.

"The Path To Wealth: Seven Spiritual Steps For Financial Abundance." By May McCarthy. San Antonio,

TX: Hierophant, 2015

"Growing Business with Soul: Practical Spirituality For The Busy Entrepreneur." By Jasmine Sampson. New Zealand: Transformational Living Publications, 2015.

ON WORK-LIFE / CAREER:

"The Art of Work: How To Make Work, Work For You." By Janice Howroyd Bryant. Torrance, CA: ASK International, 2009.

NON-MONEY BOOKS:

"Prayers for Parents." By Renee Bartkowski. Ligouri, MO: Ligouri, 2001.

"Daring Greatly: How the Courage to Be Vulnerable Transforms the Way We Live, Love, Parent, and Lead." By Brene Brown. London: Penguin UK, 2013.

"Mini Habits: Smaller Habits, Bigger Results." By Stephen Guise. Self-published, 2013 (Available at Amazon.com)

"Brain Rules: 12 Principles for Surviving and Thriving at Work, Home, and School." By John Medina. Seattle, WA: Pear Press, 2014 (Second Edition)

"Women's Bodies. Women's Wisdom (Revised Edition): Creating Physical and Emotional Health and Healing." By Christiane Northrup. New York: Bantam, 2010.

"Stone Soup." By Marcia Brown. New York, NY: Simon & Shuster, 1947.

VIDEOS:

Geese That Grow On Trees? (YouTube) https://www.youtube.com/watch?v=zWSe2qezhm4

A Tale of Two Brains (YouTube) - https://www.youtube.com/watch?v=3XjUFYxSxDk

WEBSITES:

Money Coaching Institute:

www.moneycoachinginstitute.com

Self-Made by Nely Galan: www.becomingselfmade.com

Sweet Spot Strategy with Racheal Cook:

www.sweetspotstrategy.com

The 5 Second Rule: https://melrobbins.com/5second-rule- hack-science-explained/

The Art of Money: Financial Therapy For Your Soul:

http://baritessler.com

World Wide Women: www.worldwidewomen.com

Your Best Mind: *Using the Science Behind Psychology To Train Your Brain For Greater Success in Business and Life:* www.yourbestmindonline.com

About the Author

Marlene Elizabeth is an Author, Speaker, Mamapreneur and founder of **MONEYWINGS™**. Through her books, workshops, private one-one-coaching and podcast *Let's Get Tender™: Money Conversations That Matter* (RHG-TV Network), **Marlene empowers women to** transform their money story so their financial dream can take flight.

Deeply inspired by her financial dream to raise a money-smart girl as a single stay-at-home Mom, Marlene went on to become bestselling author of ***MONEYWINGS™***: *Unfolding Your Financial Potential One Brave Feather At A Time.* Due for release on her daughter's birthday July 18, 2018, her book is a Spirit-filled love-note to help women kindle their confidence in their relationship to money, and ultimately in themselves.

For years, she questioned *"why financial dreams seemed so easy to come true for others, but not for me?"* As a financial- role model for her daughter, it became her mission to find the answer by living the question. Today, Marlene teaches life-changing strategies to breakthrough limiting beliefs around money and success to help other women who are struggling with similar questions and challenges in their relationship to money.

Her clients uncover their unique, untapped financial potential, and authentic gifts and strengths while developing a powerful sense of confidence, clarity and purpose to thrive. Marlene believes the world needs the financial dream in every woman's heart to come true.

Her book **MONEYWINGS™** has been featured in the Huffington Post, RHG Magazine & TV-Guide, Tribute Magazine, Empowering You Transforming Lives Radio, Modern Day Women podcast, Worldwide Women and The Spirited Woman Top 12 Pick.

Her next book *Embrace Your Wealth: Living A Financially Spiritual Life* is due for release April 2019. She is a featured contributing author in *Bloom Where You Are Planted and Shine; Step Forward and SHINE (November 2018); Empowering YOU, Transforming Lives 365 Daily Reflections (December 2018); and Step Into Your Brilliance (Fall 2019).*

Marlene earned her Master's degree in Religious Education from Boston College School of Theology and Ministry and

B.A. in International Relations from U.C. Davis. She is a Certified Money Coach® and Certified Brain Personality Specialist.

To learn more about Marlene's books, speaker schedule, workshops, podcast or private coaching, please visit www.marleneelizabeth.com.

MONEYWINGS™ proudly sponsored by...

New Weekly Podcast!
LET'S GET TENDER™
Money Conversations
That Matter
with Marlene Elizabeth
Premiering AUGUST 29th!
Wednesdays at 10:00 AM PST
Empowered Voices TV Channel
RHG-TV Network
www.LetsGetTender.com

Reviews

Dalena Alexandria Lyall

Wow! Takes my breath away. When I was 6 years old, my Mom wrote me a special song to teach me about money (*"ohhhh... what can you do with a cookie? I can share it, save it, grow it, or eat it"*). By comparing money to a cookie, it helped me to understand how to use my money carefully. Now my Mom is teaching others about money too. I was touched when I read that I am her "compelling why" to never give up. I am proud to share my "safe- place" with you so you can "stop doubting and start daring." Congratulations Mom on your first book!

Dalena Alexandria Lyall Author's Daughter

Elementary School - 5th Grade

Cynthia Stott

Marlene Elizabeth's book **MONEYWINGS™** is a God-send for entrepreneurs who struggle with money issues and getting their business off the ground. She is a single-mom with a unique perspective on how the inner workings of your brain and mind can hold you back and prevent you from achieving your dreams. As a global visibility influencer, I see that it is my entrepreneurial clients' mindset, especially around making money and building wealth, that holds them back most from building a business that provides the impact and financial freedom they desire. This book gives you deep insights and practical steps. It takes you on a journey from discovering your money story to changing it so that your entrepreneurial dreams can take flight.

Cynthia Stott

International Speaker Coach and Global Visibility Influencer www.CynthiaStott.com

Kristen Harper

MONEYWINGS™ is a must read for any woman who truly wants financial freedom! This book is full of truths, including mindfulness, trust your heart, tapping into your strengths, we create what we believe, and much more. Negative thoughts hidden in the subconscious mind can sabotage financial success, as well as other areas of your life. When you let go of these limiting thoughts and nurture yourself from within, the universe will begin to support your dream.

Marlene Elizabeth provides valuable tips to guide you step- by-step in making your financial dreams and life's purpose a reality.

Kristen Harper, Health and Wellness Expert
KristenHarperSpeaks.com
PerfectHealthConsultingServices.com

John Hall

Marlene Elizabeth is a revolutionary thought leader on breaking the code for those of us who languish in our money fears. She has created thought-provoking and practical methods of re-shaping negative and limiting beliefs about money.

She teaches how, through this re-shaping of thinking, one can completely turn limiting beliefs on their head. Her inspirational methods allow us to transform limiting beliefs into healthy, positive, and motivational relationships with money.

If you have ever struggled with trying to work through the myriad of standard money explanatory literature and are still not on your way to financial empowerment, then the inspiration that is embodied in Marlene's Moneywings™ is "*a must read!*

John Hall, MBA, LCDR USN (Ret) Best Selling Author, Financial Expert Sailor180@hotmail.com

Janise Graham

Along with starting and scaling a business, one of the toughest things to do for so many women is to get a full grasp of their own worth. The next challenge is having a good relationship with the monies earned.

MONEYWINGS™ is the first stepping stone in creating awareness and putting emotional steps in place so that you can soar. Marlene has created healthy and repeatable thought-provoking actions and habits to lead you towards financial freedom and success.

Janise Graham, LACP, CLTC

Entrepreneur, Speaker and Author of soon-to-be-released "Leaving In Style: From Business Success to Succession" www.LeavingInStyle.com

(Entrepreneur Insurance Services) 951.817.7526 x255

Trisha Garrett

This book is an absolute must read…over and over again! It is like a beautiful reference manual with nuggets of wisdom embedded into simple practical strategies to follow. The warmth of Marlene's heart permeates throughout the pages with support and encouragement. She believes in YOU! Read this book and you are sure to find your MONEYWINGS™!

Trisha Garrett

Life Coach, Int'l Speaker, Int'l Best-Selling Author Owner: Life You Deserve

Contact: http://www.LifeYouDeserveAcademy.com FB: http://www.facebook.com/trishagarrett77

Kimi Avary

I love the consistency with which Marlene gently and compassionately encourages the reader to take mini-step after mini-step as they open to receiving financial abundance.

Kimi Avary, M.A. Relationship Navigation Specialist http://ConsciousCouplesNetwork.com
Http://MeetWithKimi.com

Kim Schroeder-Evans

Very well written with lovely quotes, creative expression and heartfelt truths. MONEYWINGS™ is for those who are eager to continue their calling as entrepreneurs, as well as for those who might be ready to just "throw-in-the-towel" and say, "no more!" MONEYWINGS™ is a most heart- centered, supportive, encouraging and enjoyable book for new and long-time entrepreneurs; both successful and struggling, looking for positive motivation to continue to follow their dreams, "one brave feather at a time." Marlene compels us to find the "heart and soul" behind WHAT we do to earn money, HOW we make that happen and most importantly, the WHY behind all that we do. Once you begin this book, you won't want to put it down.

Kim Schroeder-Evans Professor and Tutor of Spanish kim@dixonlanguagecenter.com

Olivia Parr-Rud

If you struggle with making or managing money then this book is for you! Motivated by her desire to care for her daughter, Marlene shares her deeply personal journey of discovery and healing. She reveals powerful insights and practices that will help you re-frame and realign your relationship with money. I especially love her 8 Money Mindsets. They go way beyond just helping you attract and manage money. These 8 mindsets will help you in every area of life!

Olivia Parr-Rud, MS Corporate Love Ambassador

Contact information: olivia@oliviapr.com

Vicki Gotsis Ceraso

MONEYWINGS™ is a refreshing book as it's more about feminine financial and personal power and less about money itself, helping women to see money through fresh eyes! Sprinkled throughout with priceless 'Brave-Heart Tips', Marlene has created a book that is not only a wealth of information, a sharing of personal experiences and many 'aha' moments, but also a book with heart and a real passion to instill a different way of thinking about wealth so that we can be the mirror for our daughters and create 'money-smart' girls for generations to come. By looking at money differently, we create a new perspective which gives us the freedom to re-create our financial future. In her unique, loving and gentle way, Marlene holds her reader's hand and walks them through her life experiences and financial roadblocks to the path of mindset change which leads to financial power and ultimately personal success.

Vicki Gotsis Ceraso

Founder of SheRises Global, TogetherWeRise Global & Story&Message AccelerateHER www.sherisesglobal.com

https://www.linkedin.com/in/vicki-gotsis-ceraso-37523262/

https://www.facebook.com/vicki.ceraso Twitter: @cerasovicki instagram.com/vicki.ceraso

Email: vicki@sherisesglobal.com

Kari Kelley

MONEYWINGS™ gave me a gentle, graceful way to create a relationship with money. I am able to have compassion for myself, release shame and focus on a sustainable partnership. The simple language and the way it weaves mental, physical and spiritual connections make this book versatile.

Kari Kelley Author/Speaker Karilkelley.com
info@karilkelley.com (408) 373-7263

Carol Asper

I plan to share MONEYWINGS™ with my family, friends and clients. Marlene gives the reader a new way to think about money. She shares her perspectives in growing up and how she thought about money. Then progresses to share how she found ways to change her thinking. This book is short and to the point.

MONEYWINGS™ provide real world experiences.

Marlene shares Brave-heart tips and provides steps to achieve success not just in your thoughts about money but also in growing your business and success.

Carol Asper Financial Advisor

Carol.asper@gmail.com Cell phone: 626-922-0753

Laurie Vallas

MONEYWINGS™ - A WELCOMED CHANGE. Raw.

Vulnerable. Generous. Approachable. Viable. Up until now, 'tenderness' was not a term I would have readily associated with money. Rich with clever double-entendres; subtly adding up to a new, heart-centered financial language – MONEYWINGS™ gently transforms historically negative experiences and beliefs about money; bringing a brand-new philosophy and narrative on how 'well-th' management can be achieved.

With each emerging anecdote, not only did I find my own confidence rising, but I began to think of all the women I knew who could also relate to, and benefit from, the wisdom shared in this very personal journey of economic transformation. Marlene Elizabeth's approach – complete with her signature 'Brave-Heart-Tips' – contained several valuable lessons. The investment in the exercises is time well spent; leaving the reader with a unique sense of restored and renewed self-worth.

Laurie Vallas, Founder, The Heartifacts Publishing Email: theheartifacts@gmail.com

Facebook: Laurie Vallas – Author Instagram: theheartifacts

Adrian Jefferson Chofor

If you are looking for a book that will help you transform your relationship with money, then look no further, this book is for you! Marlene provides fresh and dynamic ways to look at our relationship with money, and in the process, take actionable steps to reach our financial dreams. In this powerful, yet easy-to-read book, she shares real life, heartwarming examples of her own struggles as an entrepreneur to gain financial independence and grow MONEYWINGS™. I would highly recommend this book to everyone, especially Mamapreneurs, and women that want to learn concepts, strategies, and tools that will give them the power to transform their financial life, so they can start living the life they want and deserve.

Adrian Jefferson Chofor

Global Expat Whisperer & Empowerment Leader
www.adrianjeffersonchofor.com

Linda Patten

MONEYWINGS™ isn't just another book telling you how to manage your finances. It's a book about reshaping your relationship with money by examining your attitudes and beliefs around money. The author takes you on the journey of her own shifting of mindset that is powerful in the telling and in the reflection on my own challenges. The story is also laced with practical practices to assist the reader to move from anxiety over money to feeling safe that are quick, easy and powerful. Marlene Elizabeth weaves in tips to unfold your financial potential and take you deeper into your relationship with money. In the end, she gives us a great summary with recommendations that answers the questions on everyone's mind. Finally, the resource section gives individuals like who want to dig even deeper a broad list of books from which to choose and reflect upon.

Leadership Trainer for Women Entrepreneurs & Changemakers, President & CEODare2Lead With Linda
www.dare2leadwithlinda.com
https://www.facebook.com/dare2leadwithlinda
https://www.facebook.com/linda.patten.311
https://twitter.com/patten_linda

https://www.linkedin.com/in/lindapatten

http://www.youtube.com/c/LindaPatten

Linda Palmer

Made in the USA
Monee, IL
04 November 2026

67388639R10075